SOCIAL & EMOTIONAL CURRICULUM FOR GIFTED STUDENTS

SOCIAL & EMOTIONAL CURRICULUM FOR GIFTED STUDENTS

Grade 3

Project-Based Learning Lessons That Build Critical Thinking, Emotional Intelligence, and Social Skills

Mark Hess

PRUFROCK PRESS INC.
WACO, TEXAS

Prufrock Press Inc.
P.O. Box 8813
Waco, TX 76714-8813
Phone: (800) 998-2208
Fax: (800) 240-0333
https://www.prufrock.com

Table of Contents

Introduction

The process of growing into one's wonderful self can be messy. The most meaningful pathways don't follow a straight line. The social and emotional lives of gifted children are wide and deep, and the journey toward self-understanding is the most essential part of teaching and learning.

Yet educators tend to think of the social-emotional aspects of giftedness as issues to be addressed, problems to overcome, or roadblocks to thriving. In moments of frustration, as teachers and parents, we might forget about one of the most essential components of giftedness—asynchronous development. Just because a gifted 6-year-old can think like a 10-year-old doesn't mean that same student should have developed the social skills of a 10-year-old. The 6-year-old, in fact, may have the social skills of a 4-year-old. Little kids with little hands may envision an engineering project well beyond their years but may not be able to handle scissors well or know how to use drafting tools or design software. These frustrations abound in the asynchronous world of gifted learners, yet these frustrations are both common and normal. We might stumble into a deficit model of thinking about these asynchronous challenges.

In these moments, I hope we don't forget the beauty of intensities—the way gifted learners tend to experience the world in a more rich and textured way, are able to make connections others cannot, and are able to create a personal poetry in this world if we only stop and listen to them. I hope we don't forget about the value of the journey itself. The lessons and units in this book offer an engaging variety of pathways for students to share their journey with teachers and with one another.

Background

I first taught elementary gifted kids in a small school district at the foot of Pikes Peak. My classroom was in the 1923 wing of the original school building. Eight-foot high windows looked out on Colorado's Front Range. The oak floor was the original floor from 1923, stained and sealed many times over into a rich brown, with black dots in perfect lines where the desks had once been bolted in place. A former second-grade teacher's name was etched into the slate blackboard in a beautiful, swooping, cursive script.

The gifted groups who came bounding down the stairs to my classroom, however, were anything but bolted in place. We worked with craft saws and hot glue, piles of cardboard, nuts and bolts, small pieces of wood, batteries, wires, and switches. We made trash bag bat wings, plaster bear paw prints created in the mud outside, marshmallow trebuchets, miniature skate parks, and an elf village populated by peanut people dressed in felt clothing. This was STEAM curriculum before anyone had used that term. This was creative graphic design when the most complicated design program available to us was Kid Pix. I remember reading learning standards from the National Association for Gifted Children (NAGC) for the first time during these years, and I thought they rang true, but the standards didn't guide my teaching. Instead, I drove to a recycling center and filled my truck with 2-liter soda bottles so my class could duct tape together a tube that would carry a tennis ball all around the room, allowing it to roll from ceiling to floor. I spent my planning time not wondering how my students would learn more about themselves as gifted learners, but dreaming up the next thematic unit and the next project.

Teaching and loving these kids helped me understand that being gifted goes far beyond creative expression and passion projects. Giftedness often means leading with the heart. My students tended to lead with their kindness and compassion, were guided by a full range of feelings and emotions, and were often very hard on themselves. Emotional intensity in the gifted is, as Sword (2011) so poetically described it, "vivid, absorbing, penetrating, encompassing, complex, commanding—a way of being quaveringly alive" (para. 3). Many of our gifted students carry a reservoir of compassion. Their storehouse has been filled by an ability to see another's perspective and to imagine another's struggle. At a young age, our gifted students begin to sort out injustices and develop a beautiful acceptance of others. This reservoir of compassion, like no other, characterizes who gifted children are and sets the course for this book.

Development of Social-Emotional Units

When my students skip, run, and sometimes even walk appropriately through my classroom doorway, they expect exciting and engaging opportunities. That's why I believe approaching the vital social-emotional components of gifted programming should never feel like a trip to the counseling office. I want to use my best teacher skills and surprise students with vibrant experiences around social-emotional understanding—experiences that are often necessarily hands-on and creative.

Some of the lessons in this book did not begin as social-emotional lessons at all but grew out of curricular projects. Some grew out of conversations with parents, students, or classroom teachers. Some grew from a perceived need, an article I was writing, or a presentation for colleagues.

Unit 1: A Precious Gift: Introduction to Social-Emotional Learning has been my introduction to giftedness to my groups for many years. The lessons set the stage for a way of *being* and *becoming* in a gifted classroom through metaphors, a hands-on approach, creativity, a sense of humor, and personalized explorations.

Unit 2: My Flag: Self-Understanding and Individuality grew from a warm-up I created for an advanced literacy group. I wanted students to practice using drafting templates and tools in a thoughtful way. At the same time, we happened to be discussing how colors evoke a psychological effect and are used in advertising, and the two concepts came together in a lesson about identity. Each year, although groups of kids come in and out of my classroom throughout the week, their flags never leave a special spot on the wall.

Unit 3: Bouncing Back: Growth Mindset grew out of a parent-teacher conference and a blog post I wrote for NAGC, "Surfing a Wave of Wonderfulness" (Hess, 2019). Most of the kids I teach are high achievers, and although they carry an impression of academic success, I wonder if they are truly thriving or have fallen into a complacency that pleases everyone else. Many of my students have not had opportunities to experience that icky feeling inside their stomachs that signals they haven't quite understood something yet. They've developed an identity as the student who finishes first and gets all of the answers correct. When they eventually fall off that wave of wonderfulness, it can be an assault on their very identity.

Unit 4: Suitcases and Circles of Hope: Identity was originally part of a thematic unit on circles. My school's third graders were in the midst of a wonderful, project-based unit on Ellis Island, and I wanted to extend the curriculum for them to a deeper, more metaphorical level than they were getting in their classrooms. About this same time in my own life, the mountain community in which I live had been placed on standby evacuation because of a nearby forest fire. With only an SUV to take our most prized possessions, my children and I had to reach a reckoning with the things we valued the most. The reckoning, in the end, came down to "Who am I, really?"—not just "What can I not live without?" but also "Why can't I live without it?" In filling their suitcases for this lesson, I hoped that students would think more deeply about the people, things, and ideas they value the most—not just the *what*, but the *who* and the *why* as well.

Finally, Unit 5: What Comes From the Heart: Empathy and Compassion represents an interaction my students and I have shared so many times. These lessons originated from a story we read about friendship and leading with one's heart, a Haitian folktale called *The*

Banza by Diane Wolkstein. After a deep and interactive discussion into the story's themes, one student wanted to know, "But when do we get to build something?" OK, I thought. Let's build a metaphor!

Teaching the Units

So how can teachers make the most profound impact in the short amount of time we have with our students? How can we engage creativity, stretch academic standards, and grow at the same time? Let's put our hearts and hands into cross-curricular projects designed to meet gifted students' thirst for self-expression. Let's provide opportunities for students to understand themselves a little better in each lesson. Each unit in this book begins with an active Launch lesson to engage gifted learners. Each unit is aligned to NAGC's (2019) Pre-K–Grade 12 Gifted Programming Standards, specifically the student outcomes from Standard 1: Learning and Development. Also included with each unit is a list of social-emotional themes addressed, as well as academic skills that will be enhanced.

I hope that you will weave these lessons in and out of your curriculum in a way that is personal to you and the children you teach. Please feel free to add, delete, or adjust to make these lessons your own. I hope that the process of growing into one's wonderful self is messy with hot glue, glitter, craft sticks, and construction paper, as well as with understanding. I hope that you and your students have as much fun and produce as many memories as mine have.

For even more engaging units for gifted learners, see the companion books in this series, *Social and Emotional Curriculum for Gifted Students: Grade 4* and *Social and Emotional Curriculum for Gifted Students: Grade 5*.

UNIT 1

A PRECIOUS GIFT
Introduction to Social-Emotional Learning

Background

Where does the conversation begin with a group of newly identified gifted learners? In this unit, students create a 3-D metaphor that serves as a vehicle for opening important conversations about giftedness. We know that addressing the social-emotional needs of gifted learners is an important part of any gifted and talented program; however, will a barrage of information about giftedness serve anyone well in the first hours of contact? Not likely.

On the first day, students are wondering what they'll do in the gifted and talented education (GATE) program. There is an excitement at hand, but a cautious one. Students are wondering:

» Why did I get pulled out of class?
» What does gifted and talented mean?
» Will I be able to keep up with everyone else in this group?

Parents are wondering what the gifted program entails and, at the same time, may be thinking back on their own experiences as gifted learners—experiences that may have been positive, negative, or very different from what their children are about to experience. At the same time, students in the regular classroom are wondering where their gifted friends are going once a week or every day when they leave with that mysterious GATE teacher.

These lessons are designed to help students begin to understand giftedness and to provide a way for young gifted learners to talk to their friends about what this "GATE stuff" is all about. This unit also serves to open an important line of communication between parents and the gifted and talented resource teacher. Furthermore, as students begin working with metaphors on the first day, they begin to see that not all questions have right or wrong answers, but supporting opinions with details lends value to understanding.

As an opening session to GATE, this unit is not meant to be a comprehensive examination of giftedness and social-emotional awareness. Rather, it will lay the groundwork for important social-emotional issues that students will return to again and again throughout their program (and most likely throughout their lives):

- » What is giftedness?
- » What is perfectionism, and does it apply to me?
- » How do I maintain friendships?
- » What can I do with my gifts and talents?

It seems appropriate to start that discussion by addressing the basic concern of defining and clarifying what giftedness is. We will continue by creating a "people" paper chain metaphor, which will help students understand giftedness and provide them with a way to talk to their friends about gifts and talents. Finally, we'll end the introduction with a bit of homework as students take their precious gift metaphor home and invite their parents to learn about what they've created in their first GATE class.

Unit Objectives

Students will:
- » understand they have been identified as gifted learners,
- » understand that giftedness is not without its challenges and does not imply that gifted learners are inherently better than others,
- » understand the great potential of giftedness, and
- » create a metaphor for giftedness.

NAGC Learning and Development Standard

1.3. Self-Understanding. Students with gifts and talents demonstrate understanding of and respect for similarities and differences between themselves and their cognitive and chronological peer groups and others in the general population.

Themes and Skills Addressed

Social-Emotional Themes

- » Identity
- » Compassion
- » Empathy
- » Perfectionism
- » Achievement
- » Social problem solving
- » Psychosocial growth

Academic Skills

- » Vocabulary in context
- » Metaphor analysis
- » Graphic design

Launch

Wrap a present, in a box of any size, in preparation for this unit's launch, and place it conspicuously in front of the room. Add a tag that says, "For my students." As you introduce yourself and say a few words about your first gifted and talented class together, students may ask what is inside the box. Here is your perfect opening for this activity.

Ask: *What do you think is inside the present?*

Hesitant, common answers will blossom with your encouragement. Encourage students to add details and be creative.

Now change things up a bit: *What is definitely not inside this present?* This opens new possibilities—possibilities for abstract and outlandish responses. Enjoy and encourage students' creative responses.

Finally, end with this question: *What if I were to tell you that only you can decide what is inside this gift?*

Leave that statement dangling. You will be delighted with the answers you'll get in this opening creative launch, and you'll get to know different students' personalities as well.

First Day of Gifted: How Did I Get Here?

On their first day, introduce students to the purpose of the GATE program: *This is the gifted and talented program. Everyone in this room has abilities and talents very few other people have. That's why we're all here together.*

Take a deep breath. Notice the perplexed looks from students. Keep moving.

Our students—and parents—come from many different experiences with giftedness. Perhaps this is the third child in the family to enter the gifted program, and it's quite likely the parents are gifted learners as well. This family knows what to expect . . . pretty much. On the flipside, some parents I've talked to over the years seem to believe their child has just been placed in a special needs program! (Well, that *is* true, after all—just not the special needs they had in mind.) Other parents have thanked me and said they feel "honored" that I've selected their child. I try to explain that their child has selected themselves and that I've simply put the paperwork together.

Having once taught middle school gifted and talented, I know there are many middle school students who do not know how they were identified for the program in elementary school. They've been bumping around the program for a few years—never knowing exactly why they were there in the first place. Even the students I've taught since second grade in the gifted program still sometimes express bafflement or misunderstanding as fourth and fifth graders. This unit is a good "home base." It's not a bad idea to return to it to check in upon occasion—or better yet, use the Dear Gifted Learner letters shared in the Conclusion of this book to continue the discussion about giftedness on a regular basis.

I recommend beginning with an explanation of how students were identified for the gifted program. I have an introductory slideshow I use every year. Identification processes are different state to state and district to district. So, without going into specific details, my slideshow mentions the testing that was completed, the basic standards used, and the identification areas of the program. I then make sure each student knows the area or areas in which they've been identified.

As we talk about testing and identification, it's hard not to talk about the numbers and percentages used to identify students for the program. Perhaps the following sample dialogue will work for you. It seems to work for me, and I use it to make an important point that gifted learners do not fit physical stereotypes:

> Students here today all scored in the 95th percentile on one or more of the tests. What does that mean? It means that if we gathered 100 kids your age, you would have scored higher on the test than 94 of them. Only five students would have done as well as you've done.
>
> Let's talk about this a little bit more. Notice that *I* didn't choose those five students. I don't go around picking students to be in my gifted and talented class. Those five students chose themselves by doing so well on the test. You chose yourself—not me! Just look around this room. Doesn't everyone look a bit different? How in the world could I pick out gifted learners when gifted learners don't look a certain way? Gifted learners might be anyone.

Lesson 1.1

What Is a Gifted Learner?

In the first lesson, students will make a "people paper chain" and label each "person" on the chain with one of five key points about being gifted. When introducing the concept of giftedness, keep it simple to start. Third graders don't need textbook discussions from our licensing programs. As students continue in the GATE program, you can add depth to the question of what being a gifted learner means. For the time being, focus on helping students understand the five key points in this lesson:

1. I have a precious gift.
2. Everyone is special in some way.
3. Nobody is perfect.
4. I can use my talents to achieve many things.
5. I can use my talents to help others.

Materials

» Handout 1.1: Paper Chain Template
» 11" x 18" sheets of white copy paper (one per student)
» Scissors
» Pens, markers, and colored construction paper (optional)

Estimated Time

» 40 minutes

Preparation

>> Using a sheet of white copy paper, these chains make four people from left to right. Counting the front and the back sides of the paper, each sheet provides eight people to write messages on. Students will write the five points on the people that make up the chain, leaving three extra for more personal items.

>> I managed to grow up without ever knowing how to make a paper chain! There are many good video instructions online—better than I can provide in this text. (A couple of examples include: https://www.youtube.com/watch?v=pocc2DdmrF4 and https://www.youtube.com/watch?v=O2A15vwcR-Q). Handout 1.1: Paper Chain Template includes a cutout of the paper person for students' use.

>> Construction paper will be very difficult to cut—especially with kid scissors. Plain copy paper is recommended.

>> Students should leave one of the people on the chain blank for the time being. This should be the front of the chain when it is folded. Students will decorate this space to look like themselves, but this task should be saved until the final step (see Figure 1). That way students can take their time on the rest of the chain and will not be distracted from the social-emotional lessons added to the other seven people in the chain.

Procedure

Distribute one sheet of 11" x 18" copy paper to each student. Using the guidance from the previous section, have students cut out their paper chains. Once students have cut out their paper chains, have them begin filling it with the five social-emotional key points.

Key Point 1: I Have a Precious Gift. On one paper person (it doesn't matter which—just not the front), students should write, "I have a precious gift." See Figure 2 for an example.

Encourage students to discuss Key Point 1. Your facilitation as a teacher will lend personality to these discussions, but let the students' interests guide the direction of the dialogue. As a facilitator, reframe questions, ask for clarification, and keep the discussion focused. Try not to supply the answers.

The following are suggested discussion points; however, add your own ideas as you see fit:

>> Why do we use the word *precious*? What does *precious* mean?

>> Can someone simply state, "OK, from now on I'm going to try really, really hard to be gifted"?

>> Gifted learners' brains are "wired" for giftedness just like the fastest runners' lean, powerful muscles are wired for fast-twitch responses. What are similarities and differences between gifted learners and great athletes?

>> Let's say you gave a precious gift to someone on their birthday. How would you feel if they didn't appreciate or want that gift?

>> All precious items come in different shapes, forms, and sizes. Giftedness comes in many forms. Is it possible to be gifted in every way?

Figure 1
Cover Chain Example

Check out this personalized cover for this student's people chain. The skirts match! Save this activity for last, though. It's the most time consuming, and students can easily get distracted with it.

Key Point 2: Everyone Is Special in Some Way. On their second paper person, students should write "Everyone is special in some way." A student's identification for the gifted program can be a sticky business. Students worry about leaving their friends behind. Parents worry about being unfairly branded as elitist. Sometimes teachers don't know exactly what to say to either the students in the program or the students who have not been identified. Being identified as a gifted learner can almost make one feel guilty: *Why did I get this gift and others did not?* Gifted kids—with full hearts and compassionate souls—want all of their friends to be included, too. Just take a look one of Galbraith's (2013) "8 Great Gripes of GT Kids" that is related to these concerns: "6. Our friends and classmates don't always understand us, and they don't see all of our different sides" (p. 24).

Every year, a student is bound to ask, "But isn't everyone gifted?" No doubt an adult in their life has said this, and it stuck. Isn't this the generous and modest response to giftedness, after all? Certainly, but that doesn't make it true. Because gifted program specialists are charged with helping guide social-emotional well-being in our students, we need to address the belief that everyone is gifted. We can do so with an equally generous and modest—but

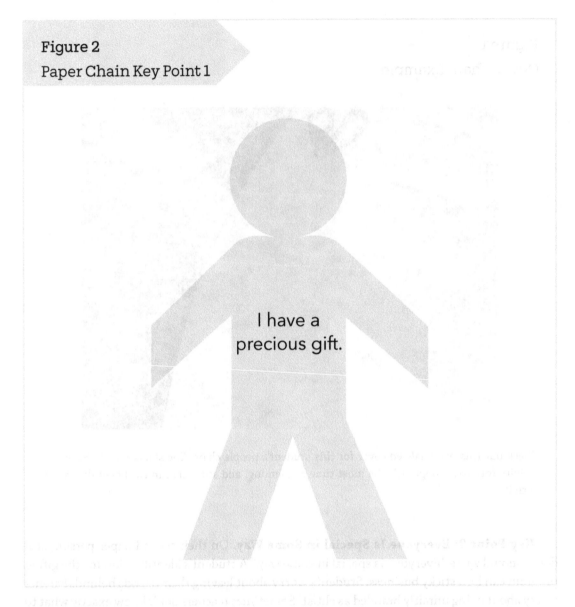

Figure 2
Paper Chain Key Point 1

I have a
precious gift.

much more truthful—statement to replace it: *Everyone is special in some way*. See Figure 3 for an example.

Questions to discuss with students might include:

» In your own words, how were you all identified as gifted learners?
» Are gifted learners the only good people in the world?
» Does being a gifted learner mean that you are also a kind person?
» Are any two people alike?
» Are differences good?
» What makes a good person?

Key Point 3: Nobody Is Perfect. The third statement for students to write on their paper chain is "Pobody is nerfect" (see Figure 4). Students will think this is pretty amusing.

Figure 3
Paper Chain Key Point 2

Everyone is special in some way.

Surprisingly, many of them will not have heard this particular spoonerism before. (Bonus discussion: What is a *spoonerism*? Have students think of other examples.)

In my 30-plus years of teaching, I've noticed that perfectionism seems to be one of the most difficult social-emotional topics. One reason is that the students who need perfectionism lessons the most are also the least likely to admit they are perfectionists—because doing so is admitting they are less than perfect! The first time I taught this lesson, one of my second graders had trouble writing "Pobody is nerfect." He erased and tried again and still got it wrong. He tried one more time and ended up erasing a hole in the paper . . . at which point he announced that he was stupid and crawled underneath his desk where he began to cry. As Yogi Berra once said, "You can observe a lot by just watching." Aside from the perfectionism, this is an example of asynchronicity in gifted learners. This student was highly gifted, preferred to be around adults, and could read and calculate on the middle school level. His fine motor skills, however, were less than that of a second grader, and his social skills were akin to

Figure 4
Paper Chain Key Point 3

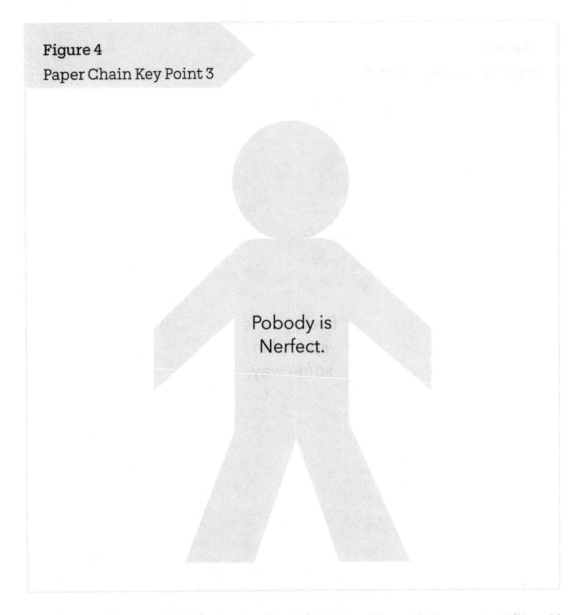

Pobody is
Nerfect.

those of younger students. What he envisioned for his paper chain, his fine motor skills could not match. He ended up with a hole in the paper and tears of frustration.

Perfectionism is a common trait in gifted learners and one of the eight great gripes of gifted students: "Parents, teachers, and even our friends expect too much of us. We're supposed to get A's and do our best all the time" (Galbraith, 2013, p. 24). Questions to discuss with students might include:

» Can you think of a time when you could laugh at yourself for not being perfect?

» Are there things in your family that brothers or sisters are better at doing than you are? How about the other way around?

» Describe something you weren't good at in the beginning but are getting better at now.

» Someone once said that there is no such thing as failure—only learning. What does this mean?
» Why do people sometimes get upset when they don't do well? What would you say to them?

Key Point 4: I Can Use My Talents to Achieve Great Things. We hope to help our students realize their academic potential, to be productive, to understand their strengths, and to do great things in life. Our conversation begins here.

As teachers, parents, and counselors, we know the messages we communicate are very important. If we praise students for being gifted, we send a message that it is the giftedness that counts. In other words, we communicate that success has little to do with a student's effort. If we praise effort, on the other hand, we recognize and value a number of good qualities: stick-to-itiveness, dedication, creative application of talents, and a willingness to fail.

Have students write the key point "I can use my talents to achieve great things" on their paper chain (see Figure 5). Tell students: *Yes, we are gifted learners, but we were given a gift that produced this potential, and it is a precious gift indeed. Behaviors and effort are what counts—no matter what is on the inside. Trying and failing is a part of growing because "pobody is nerfect" and should never be expected to be.*

Questions to discuss with students might include:
» What makes a good student?
» What makes a good learner, and is this different from being a good student?
» How would your teacher answer those questions?
» How would a parent answer those questions?
» Do you know any stories of people who used their talents to succeed? Homework challenge: Share one of those stories with the class.

Key Point 5: I Can Use My Talents to Help Others. Gifted students may express their concern about the many problems in the world yet feel helpless to do anything about these problems. Recognizing and validating this feeling is a good place to begin. Caring people feel this kind of helplessness. Compassionate people try to help others every day.

In a room full of 8- or 9-year-olds, where does one begin this discussion involving a large, complex world? Parents have shared many stories with me over the years about how their child wants to feed every homeless person they see, how a trip to the animal shelter was a traumatic journey, or how their child cried for tsunami or earthquake victims. Our gifted learners' emotional intensities are both exquisite and challenging.

Have students write the key point "I can use my talents to help others" on their paper chain (see Figure 6) as you begin discussion of these difficult topics. Feeling overwhelmed can be quite distressing for gifted students. Feeling good about ways to help others—right now, right here, today—can ease the burden. There are plenty of good opportunities to help others inside one's own school. Furthermore, one of the most basic ways to develop leadership skills is to become involved. My school has a "green" club that devotes time to collecting recyclables throughout the school and posting messages reminding students to collect items that might be donated to the cause. Student council helps coordinate entertaining events for all students as well as a canned food drive. Students might volunteer at a local pet shelter or

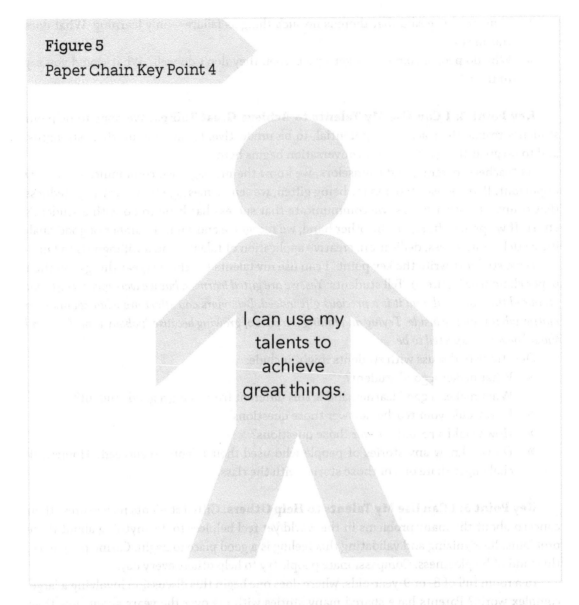

Figure 5
Paper Chain Key Point 4

I can use my talents to achieve great things.

senior center. Boy scouts, girl scouts, and other youth groups are often involved in some sort of service project. Any of these groups are a great place to begin for elementary students with an impulse to help others.

More broadly, many occupations are service-oriented, including teaching (hooray for us!). Can students name other occupations that serve others? How about medicine? It takes considerable talent and hard work to become a physician. Many of our doctors are gifted learners. Here is a good opportunity to emphasize the effort and dedication it takes—along with the talent—to be successful in a profession like medicine.

Questions to discuss with students might include:

» What are some ways students in this school help others?
» Describe an activity you've been involved in that helped other people.
» What careers are involved with helping other people?
» Why can it be difficult when we want to help other people?

Figure 6
Paper Chain Key Point 5

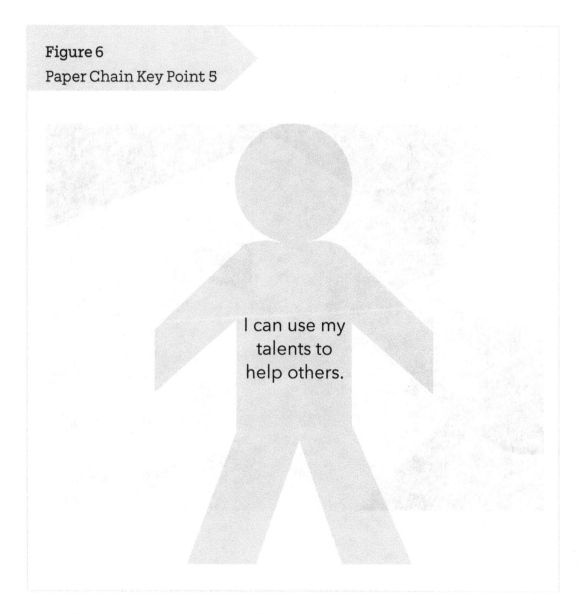

I can use my
talents to
help others.

See Figure 7 for an example of a student's paper chain.

Follow-Up: Personalization of the Paper Chain

With students' personalized cover for their paper chain and their five labels, they still have two blank "people" left to label. Encourage students to add details to these remaining spaces that show their talents.

My school district typically identifies GATE students for verbal, quantitative, or general intellectual ability, so I ask students to place their identification area or areas on one of the remaining spaces. With the one space that remains, suggest that students write something that is important to them. You might get responses like "family," "cats," and "baseball."

Figure 7
Example Paper Chain

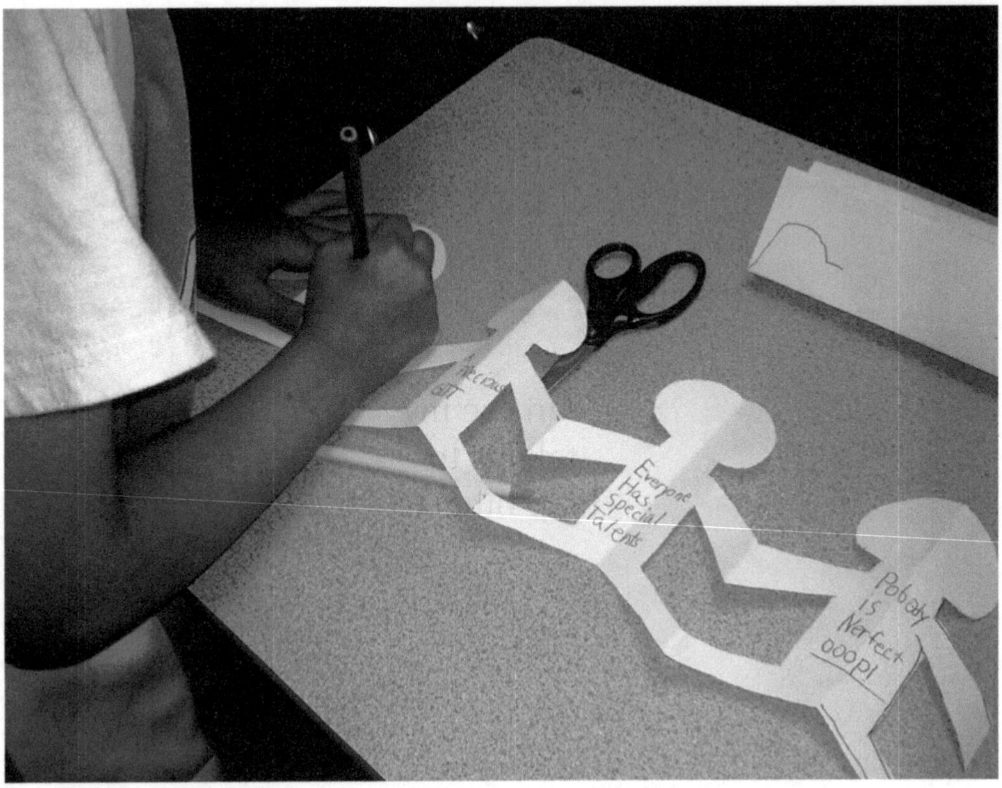

Handout 1.1

Paper Chain Template

Directions: Trace this template onto folded paper to reduce frustration and to create consistent "people"–leaving plenty of room to add decorations and labels.

Role-Playing Conversations About Giftedness

Role-play is an excellent way to practice social situations. In the process of role-playing, students process real-life situations, generate solutions, and meet conflict in a nonthreatening way. By playing a role, students remove personal doubts and fears. It's much easier to solve social problems when you are pretending to be someone else. According to Sumners and Hines (2020), creative dramatics:

> stimulates thinking, problem solving, and imagination, while encouraging awareness and concentration, helps develop emotional self-control, strengthens self-confidence in speaking and performing, develops individuality, enhances knowledge and understanding, provides insight, relies on key content, and provides opportunity for informal formative assessment of student knowledge. (p. 7)

This activity helps students prepare empathetic responses to classmates who don't understand why not everyone gets to be in the gifted program. I've experienced this social situation over and over as the gifted resource teacher: A tiny, soft-spoken, and wide-eyed child approaches me on the playground: "Why can't I be in your classes?" Although I have answered this question a hundred ways a thousand different times over the years, it still doesn't make it any easier. I wish I could work with every child, but that's not the job I chose and love. We can't expect our students to be any more immune to the emotions attached to similar questions from their classmates. In fact, we don't really want them to be—as part of the beauty of giftedness is the ability to compassionately understand the viewpoints of others.

Students in the gifted program often express enthusiasm over the challenging and creative activities that are a part of their curriculum, and other students want that same enthusiasm for what they are doing. The gifted group is the perfect place to practice responses to these uncomfortable situations.

Estimated Time

» 30 minutes

Procedure

Present the following statements to the whole class. Ask students to take a minute or two to think silently about responses to the questions that would be kind and humble yet honest at the same time:
» I wish I could go to gifted and talented classes, too.
» Why doesn't everyone go to GATE?
» I heard you guys do cool stuff in your gifted group.
» You're such a brain! You do everything right.
» I guess I'm just not good enough to be in GATE.

Now group students into triads. For each statement, one student will role-play a classmate, one student will simply be themselves and respond to the statement, and one student will be the observer. Have students switch roles with each statement.

After statements are made and responses are generated, it's the observer's responsibility to review what they saw and heard and how these things made them feel. Emphasize that observers are not judging or grading the responses. They are simply stating what they saw, heard, and how they felt as an observer.

After all of the statements are role-played, review each one with the entire class, with volunteers role-playing as the classmate and the responder. As a group, review what was seen, heard, and the feelings that were generated.

Note that no response is perfect and that there are many responses; however, here are a few suggestions for responses if the class struggles to generate effective ones:
» I wish I could go to gifted and talented classes, too: *I am really lucky to be in GATE. But, you know, everyone is special in some way. I wouldn't be in the gifted soccer program!*
» Why doesn't everyone go to GATE?: *I did really well on some tests they gave us. You're good at a lot of things, too!*
» I heard you guys do cool stuff in your gifted group: *Sometimes we do. In some ways I'm lucky to do the projects we do in GATE, but they are difficult, too. Plus, sometimes I still have to come back to class and make up things I missed.*
» You're such a brain! You do everything right: *I'm lucky I can learn new things fast. That doesn't make me better than anybody else. There are a lot of things I'm not all that great at doing, like _____. What would you say you're best at doing?*
» I guess I'm just not good enough to be in GATE: *You are special in a bunch of ways. That's why you're my friend. I like the way you _____. I go to GATE because I have a special talent for school subjects. It's just the way I am.*

Lesson 1.3

The Precious Gift Metaphor

With the paper chains complete, each student is ready to add their paper chains to their own gift box. Once assembled, students will use the gift box and paper chain as a visual aid to discuss the metaphor they've created.

Materials

» Handout 1.3: A Precious Gift Metaphor
» Handout 1.3: A Precious Gift Metaphor Sample
» Paper chains
» Gift box (one per student): Typically, I've used takeout containers of the style one usually gets at a Chinese restaurant. They can be purchased in bulk online and are inexpensive. Your local restaurant might even donate a class set. See Figure 8 for an example.

Estimated Time

» 30 minutes

Procedure

Ask students why they would want to place their people chain inside a gift box. They'll have many ideas and, most importantly, will begin to think metaphorically.

Students can use the ready-to-use activity sheet, Handout 1.3: A Precious Gift Metaphor, as a guide for discussion. In this way, students begin working with higher order thinking skills

22

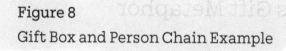

Figure 8
Gift Box and Person Chain Example

right away in the gifted and talented program. Sample responses are provided on the page following the handout.

Metaphors also give students an excellent opportunity to discuss questions that do not have one correct answer. Ask students to support their answers with explanations. Some students have little experience with metaphors or with questions that have multiple answers. Be careful to make sure no answer is rejected by anyone else in the classroom and to communicate that "correct" responses are answers that can be explained and supported with details.

Handout 1.3

A Precious Gift Metaphor

Directions: For each detail on the left, write what it makes you think of for gifted learners on the right.

Detail	Relationship to Gifted Learners
Gift Box	
People	
People Chain	
Oops! These aren't perfect cutouts.	

NAME:_____ DATE:_____

Handout 1.3

A Precious Gift Metaphor Sample

Directions: For each detail on the left, write what it makes you think of for gifted learners on the right.

Detail	Relationship to Gifted Learners
Gift Box	*We have been given a precious gift and talent as gifted learners. It is ours alone, and we get to choose how we use our gift.*
People	*Everyone is special in some way, but not everyone is a gifted learner. Our gifts are inside of us, and they are only one part of what makes us special.*
People Chain	*Our gifts and talents are not the only thing unique about us. Other qualities and interests make us shine, too. We can help others with our talents.*
Oops! These aren't perfect cutouts.	*No one can expect to be perfect or good at everything. Goofing and growing are important parts of life for everyone—gifted learners included.*

Reflecting and Sharing a Precious Gift

It's common that parents aren't exactly sure what the gifted and talented program will include. The end of this unit is a great opportunity to introduce yourself and your program and open a line of communication. This take-home activity allows students to review what they've learned in class and share important ideas with their parents or guardians. In explaining the "precious gift" to parents, students will summarize and extend their understanding. Engaged parents will add to the understanding, ask questions, and comment. In this way, parents will be invited to be involved.

Materials

- » Introductory Letter
- » Student gift boxes and paper chains

Estimated Time

- » 5 minutes, plus at-home sharing and presentations

Procedure

Inside each student's gift box, place a form inviting parents or caregivers to share their email addresses (see the Introductory Letter on the following page).

Instruct students to take the Introductory Letter home for parents to complete. Students should also present their gift boxes and paper chains to their parents, explaining what they have learned about giftedness and their own "precious gifts" in this unit.

When the forms are returned, create an email list for handy communication and follow up with a message to parents as well as an invitation to a parent information meeting. Ask parents if their child shared the precious gift activity and whether parents have any questions. I usually get great responses from the parents along with questions, and this activity has served as an excellent opener for my program over the years.

Introductory Letter

Dear Parents,

Welcome to the gifted and talented program.

This *Precious Gift* activity is the first your child will complete in an engaging and challenging program.

Please ask your child to explain their learning from this activity to you. What do the "people chain" and gift box mean? What is the importance of each message written on the chain?

As a convenient means of communicating during the school year, please either send me your email address electronically, or return this form. I will reply with an introduction and answer any questions you have.

This is always one of my favorite times of the school year—opening up a new world of learning and new experiences with wonderful kids!

My email address: _____

Your email address: _____

Sincerely,

_____

UNIT 2

MY FLAG
Self-Understanding and Individuality

Background

This unit brings best practices in 21st-century learning, critical thinking, and NAGC Learning and Development standards together in one place. Use these lessons with gifted learners for a rich experience in public speaking that meets core standards and as a study in metaphors and psychological associations that people make with colors.

Unit Objectives

Students will:
- » identify personal qualities that stand out and express their unique individuality, and
- » provide details and/or stories from their lives to illustrate their personal qualities.

NAGC Learning and Development Standards

1.3. Self-Understanding. Students with gifts and talents demonstrate understanding of and respect for similarities and differences between themselves and their cognitive and chronological peer groups and others in the general population.

1.5. Cognitive, Psychosocial, and Affective Growth. Students with gifts and talents demonstrate cognitive growth and psychosocial skills that support their talent development as a result of meaningful and challenging learning activities that address their unique characteristics and needs.

Themes and Skills Addressed

Social-Emotional Theme
- » Identity

Academic Skills
- » Metaphor analysis
- » Extemporaneous speaking
- » Explanatory writing (optional)
- » Graphic design

Launch

Prepare in advance by gathering information about your state/province flag's meaning (or, alternatively, assign the gathering of information as a background project to your students).

In preparation for an introductory discussion, project an image of the flag for your state or province for students to see. Begin by encouraging students to connect ideas with the symbols and colors on a flag. For example, for Colorado's state flag (see Figure 9), you might present the following:

Did you know that the colors on a flag represent different ideas?
- » The blue on the Colorado flag represents the blue skies. Colorado has blue skies and sunshine 300 days a year.
- » The gold in the middle is the Colorado sun. Some say it represents the gold found in the Colorado gold rush of 1859.
- » The white is the snow-capped mountains. Colorado is famous for its Rocky Mountain snowy peaks and skiing.
- » The red of the "C" represents the red soil of Colorado. In Spanish, *Colorado* literally means "red color." The Spaniard explorers named this region for its red soil.

Figure 9
Colorado State Flag

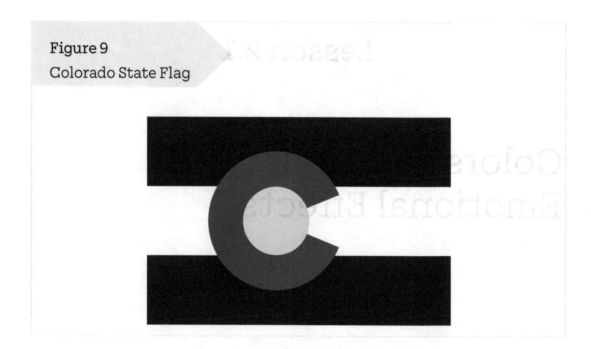

Colors and Their Emotional Effects

This lesson will help students understand that colors are much more than pigments or reflections we see. As humans, we react to colors and associate colors with feelings and impressions.

Materials

- » Handout 2.1: How Do You Feel About Colors?
- » Handout 2.1: Colors in Me
- » Handout 2.1: Colors in Me Sample

Estimated Time

- » 30 minutes

Procedure

Introduce the metaphorical and symbolic attributes of colors by distributing or displaying Handout 2.1: How Do You Feel About Colors? Examine a number of colors and their associated feelings with students. For example, you might ask:
- » Why would an advertisement for an amusement park use the color yellow? Would the color red send a different message in the same advertisement?
- » What if the classroom were painted black? How might this effect the mood inside the room?

After a discussion to check for understanding, students will make connections between colors and themselves using the graphic organizer in Handout 2.1: Colors in Me. This tool will get students ready to make a flag representing their unique qualities. Sample responses appear on the page following the handout.

Handout 2.1

How Do You Feel About Colors?

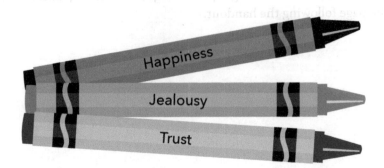

Colors make us *think* of certain things, and different colors tend to make us *feel* different ways. Decorators, designers, and advertisers have long used colors and the feelings associated with them for designs. If a decorator wants someone to feel at ease, they will choose a color that feels peaceful and relaxing, like blue. If an advertiser wants someone to see the power of their product, they will choose one of the bold colors that suggest feelings of power, like red.

Sometimes colors make us think of certain things because of what we see around us in nature. Blue makes us think of clear skies—a peaceful feeling. Green makes us think of nature and the living and healthy things in it. Red makes us think of danger. Many poisonous animals, for example, have red colors.

The following are common ways each color can make us feel.

Red excitement, power, energy, love, danger, strength, heat	**Green** nature, jealousy, healthy, lucky, new
Pink love, tenderness, calm, romantic, young	**Purple** spiritual, royal, wise, cruel, mysterious
Yellow hope, friendship, happiness, cowardice, dishonesty	**Black** evil, fear, death, power, elegant, wealthy, mystery
Blue calm, stable, peace, loyalty, sadness, trust	**Gold** wealth, success, luxury, purity
White pure, simple, clean, cold, exact, young	**Orange** social, welcoming, creative, independent, warmhearted

Handout 2.1

Colors in Me

Directions: Use Handout 2.1: How Do You Feel About Colors? to find three colors that reflect your personality and interests. Use the organizer below to help you explain and provide examples.

Color Matching Your Personality or Interests	Quality Shared by Yourself and the Color	Example or Supporting Story to Explain

Draft a flag idea using the colors you've chosen. Use large geometric shapes for the flag.

Social and Emotional Curriculum for Gifted Students, Grade 3 © Prufrock Press Inc.

NAME:_____ DATE: _____

Handout 2.1

Colors in Me Sample

Directions: Use Handout 2.1: How Do You Feel About Colors? to find three colors that reflect your personality and interests. Use the organizer below to help you explain and provide examples.

Color Matching Your Personality or Interests	Quality Shared by Yourself and the Color	Example or Supporting Story to Explain
Blue	Loyalty	Friends are really important to me, and I won't let them down.
Purple	Spiritual	I write poetry, and some people say poems are mystical.
Yellow	Hope	I am always trying to see the good in things and people.

Draft a flag idea using the colors you've chosen. Use large geometric shapes for the flag.

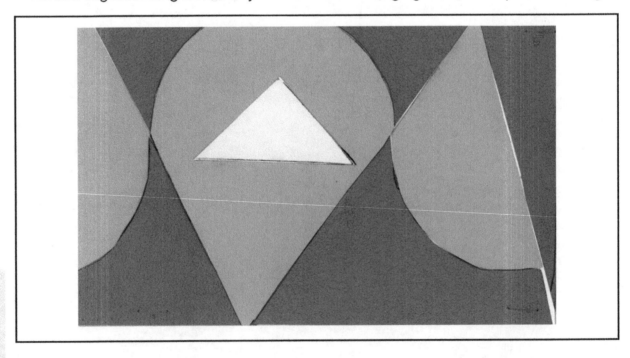

Lesson 2.2

Creating Student Flags

What if we could all design and fly a personal flag—a flag that stands for our unique personality and abilities? In this lesson, students will design their own flag, choosing colors that represent their most important qualities.

Materials

- » 5" x 8" notecards (one per student)
- » Construction paper in various colors
- » Glue and scissors
- » Items to make flags: T-squares, rulers, geometric drawing templates, and compasses
- » Pattern tools: lids, tangram sets, and French curves (optional)

Estimated Time

- » 30 minutes

Procedure

Tell students: *Rather than just drawing freehand and coloring a flag, let's make neat, colorful flags that require both planning and visual-spatial skills in graphic design.* Distribute materials to students. Each should receive a 5" x 8" notecard for the base. Students might use T-squares, rulers, geometric drawing templates, and compasses to make flags. Other items, like lids, tangram sets, and French curves, are great pattern tools as well.

Instead of simply drawing and coloring directly onto the notecards to create a flag, instruct students to cut shapes and designs from colored construction paper and glue the designs in place onto their notecards. This method creates sharp edges to designs and assures richer colors. First, students should trace the flag's design elements—a triangle and a star, for example—onto construction paper and cut them out. Students can then glue these elements onto their white notecards. If students choose white as one of their flag's colors, explain that the notecard is a ready-made background for any white they may want to appear on their flag.

Figure 10 shows a few samples of students flags.

Figure 10
Student Flag Examples

This student's flag shows a strong, loyal friend (red, yellow, blue).

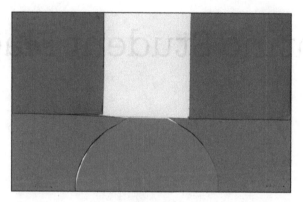

Health, power, and energy (black, red, and green): This student loves sports.

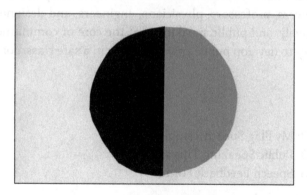

Here is the flag for simple soul who believes in love, peace, and stability (red, white, and blue). The white background from the notecard was used for the white.

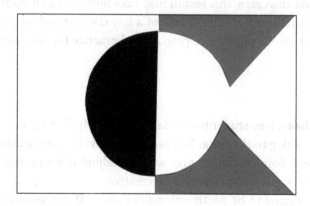

Lesson 2.3

Presenting Student Flags

Many of our gifted learners will enter careers in which they must clearly present their ideas to others. Lawyers, professors, physicians, engineers, and designers of all types must communicate effectively, and public speaking is at the core of communication success. Let's take this opportunity to develop public speaking skills in a safe classroom atmosphere.

Materials

- » Handout 2.3: My Flag Speech Template
- » Handout 2.3: Public Speaking Tips and Tricks
- » Handout 2.3: Speech Feedback Forms

Estimated Time

- » Depending on class size, this lesson may take more than an hour. I suggest breaking up the presentations over the course of a few class periods if you have a large class. Allow at least 30–45 minutes to prepare and practice for the speeches.

Procedure

Prepare Speeches. Have students use Handout 2.3: My Flag Speech Template to prepare a presentation of their flag to the class. This template provides easy access to speech planning for reluctant speakers. Some students may want to adjust the wording in the template for more flair. By all means, encourage them to be creative.

The speech is designed to be partly extemporaneous. If students are more comfortable writing their speech word for word, then allow them to. This may be one of their first times

40

speaking with an outline or template. They'll become more skilled as they become more confident as well.

Practice. Have students practice with partners before they deliver the speech. Review the guidelines on Handout 2.3: Public Speaking Tips and Tricks together as a whole class. Students should identify areas they need to practice before delivering their speech.

Deliver Speeches. Have students deliver their speeches. Distribute Handout 2.3 Speech Feedback Forms for students to take notes while others are presenting.

As mentioned previously, you may choose to have large classes spread their presentations across several class periods. Having spent more than a decade as a public speaking teacher, I've found 5–7 speeches to be an ideal number of presentations for any one sitting. Too many presentations risks losing audience focus, and we need attentive classmates for friendly and emotionally safe public speaking experiences. To encourage active listening, invite classmates of the speaker to provide an additional story about the speaker that supports one of the qualities the speaker has identified in themselves. Here is a good chance to build self-esteem.

Because public speaking can be stressful or even frightening, trust your instincts with students who seem to feel great anxiety. Although gifted and talented classes are important places to be challenged and grow, these classes are—most importantly—meant to be safe places in which all gifted students are accepted and nurtured. Likewise, feedback forms should allow only positive comments at this point. As teachers, we hope to build public speaking success early on in our classrooms. For this reason, the speech should be ungraded and celebrated as a success.

Follow-Up: Wrapping Up the Unit

Display the student flags in the classroom. You may also want to include a student's picture alongside each flag.

These flags are a good reference point throughout the year. You might casually ask a student: *Can you tell me again why you picked those colors for your flag?* This allows them to connect and reconnect with the content.

At the end of the school year, return to the flags for a check-in. Ask students:

» Do you still feel the same way about yourselves?
» What would you add to your flags?
» How have you grown this year?

Handout 2.3

My Flag Speech Template

Directions: Use the following template to help you organize and deliver your speech. Use the longer lines to write notes about personal experiences that illustrate why each quality is true in you. Do not write complete sentences. Each short story should only be about 15 seconds in length when you present it.

Hello, I am _____, and this is my flag [*Hold up flag*].

(name)

[*Point to color on flag*] _____ stands for _____ .

(first color)   (quality the color represents)

One example is: _____

_____ .

[*Point to flag again*] _____ is another color I've chosen because I am

(second color)

_____ .

(quality the color represents)

One example is: _____

_____ .

The last color is _____ . This represents _____ .

(third color)   (quality this last color represents)

One example is: _____

_____ .

Just like my flag, I am _____ , _____ , and _____ .

(first color)   (second color)   (third color)

Do you see any of these qualities in me?

Handout 2.3

Public Speaking Tips and Tricks

Directions: Consider the following advice for delivering a successful speech. Which of these tips might you practice before you present your flag?

» In public speaking, use your voice and gestures to emphasize key points and to keep your audience interested.

» Can everyone in the room hear you? If not, you just lost part of your audience.

» Don't let your flag distract the audience. Hold it up only when you are referring to it directly.

» You'll never need a partner or assistant for this speech. Let your friends support you by being a good listener in the audience.

» Stay on track. Your job as speaker is to prove one main idea, and one main idea only, with examples and explanations. In such a short speech, you have no room to talk about anything else. It's like a good paragraph.

» Do not write out supporting details. This is a speech, not an essay. Work out what you will say through rehearsing the speech.

» Rehearse. Rehearse again.

» Look at your audience as much as possible, and make sure you're not staring at one person the whole time. (Now that would be awkward!) Some people feel shy about looking at the audience. If that is difficult for you, look just barely over the top of their heads at the back wall. Your audience will never know the difference.

» Be you. Use your personality. Use your voice.

» Be confident. Everyone is in the same situation. Take a deep breath. Rehearse some more. Take another deep breath. You'll do fine!

NAME:_____ DATE: _____

Handout 2.3

Speech Feedback Forms

My Flag Speech　　　　Speaker's Name _____

One good thing I noticed:

The part I liked the best:

Sincerely, _____

My Flag Speech　　　　Speaker's Name _____

One good thing I noticed:

The part I liked the best:

Sincerely, _____

My Flag Speech　　　　Speaker's Name _____

One good thing I noticed:

The part I liked the best:

Sincerely, _____

UNIT 3

BOUNCING BACK
Growth Mindset

Background

  This unit is appropriate either for whole-class enrichment or specifically as a gifted learner's unit. Its lessons are universal to all learners, and, with guidance from the teacher, the challenges can be met on differing ability levels. The extension at the end of the unit is more specifically designed for advanced and gifted learners in third grade.

  In *Mindset: The New Psychology of Success*, Dweck (2006/2016) explained that a growth mindset—believing one's talents and abilities can be nurtured, developed, and enhanced—is a means to foster achievement and success. Resilience is a strong part of a growth mindset. The ability to bounce back, persevere, try again, and regroup to meet perceived setbacks is key to a growth mindset. Sometimes gifted learners have not been challenged at the appropriate levels. One consequence of this lack of challenge is that gifted learners can be literally unfamiliar with the uncomfortable feelings associated with struggling to learn and find answers to difficult problems. Not only do gifted learners expect learning to come easily, as it always has, but also when confronted with a difficult task, they may shut down or avoid that task—sometimes in very creative ways. Gifted learners, so often praised for their effortless mastery, may feel assaulted on a personal level: *What has happened to me? I thought I was gifted. Maybe*

I'm not smart anymore. For these reasons, social-emotional lessons about resilience and perfectionism are a key component to gifted programming.

All teachers discuss setting goals, trying hard, and seeing unsuccessful attempts as a pathway to success. This lesson in this unit addresses resilience specifically, but it should not stand in isolation from the other components of a growth mindset, like goal setting, or from continued support and guidance from caring mentors. Teachers using this unit may have already spoken about resilience with their students. All the better! This lesson will work as either an introduction to, or a reinforcing challenge for, understanding the important behaviors and mindsets for resilience.

Unit Objectives

Students will:
- » understand that resilience is an important part of growth and success, and
- » create messages to encourage growth for themselves and their classmates.

NAGC Learning and Development Standards

1.2. Self-Understanding. Students with gifts and talents possess a developmentally appropriate understanding of how they learn and grow; they recognize the influences of their beliefs, traditions, and values on their learning and behavior.

1.5. Cognitive, Psychosocial, and Affective Growth. Students with gifts and talents demonstrate cognitive growth and psychosocial skills that support their talent development as a result of meaningful and challenging learning activities that address their unique characteristics and needs.

Themes and Skills Addressed

Social-Emotional Themes
- » Goal setting
- » Growth mindset
- » Resilience
- » Psychosocial development

Academic Skills
- » Inferences
- » Collaborative discussion
- » Metaphor analysis
- » Metaphor creation
- » Data collection/analysis
- » Fractions
- » Measurement
- » Dividing decimals
- » Percentages

Figure 11

Circus Poster Image

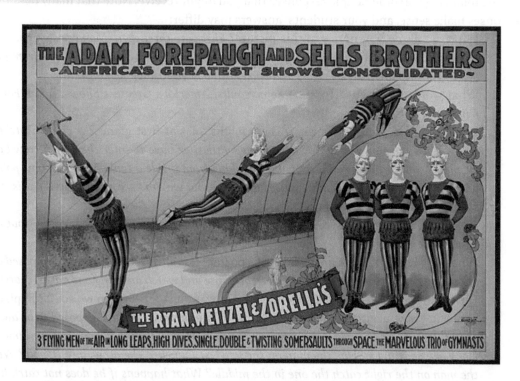

"The Adam Forepaugh and Sells Brothers, America's Greatest Shows Consolidated—The Ryan, Weitzel & Zorella's," circa 1898, Buffalo, NY, Courier Litho. Co. United States Library of Congress Prints and Photographs Division. https://www.loc.gov/pictures/item/2007682627

Launch

Use the circus poster in Figure 11 to engage students and launch the lesson. This poster is a part of the wonderful digital prints and photographs collection from the U.S. Library of Congress. You may access the image at the web address shown in the picture credits and display the image for students to analyze.

First, engage students with observations, and then extend these observations into making inferences about the poster. Use the following discussion questions to lead students through the process:

1. What details do you notice in this picture?
2. What words stand out?
3. What details do you notice that others might miss at first glance?
4. What part of the picture stands out?
5. What do you think is the purpose of this poster?

6. How does the artist who designed this poster want us to feel when we see it? Explain how you know using details and words from the picture.

The following are some sample responses that you might receive. Note that many possible responses make sense, and your students' answers may differ:

1. What details do you notice in this picture? *There are three men. Men are swinging on bars and cables. One of them seems to be suspended in the air. A clown watches from far below. The men are wearing tights and makeup and have strange-looking hair.*

2. What words stand out? *Twisting Somersaults. America's Greatest Shows. Adam Forepaugh and Sells Brothers.*

3. What details do you notice that others might miss at first glance? *A crowd watches from below. The crowd is so tiny and far away that we have to infer they are a crowd of people watching. The crowd is probably watching from inside a tent. Are those tent poles and canvas? There are probably circus rings below, but we can't see a full ring. What is the square object between the rings?*

4. What part of the picture stands out? *The man flying through the air and reaching out to another man hanging upside down.*

5. What do you think is the purpose of this poster? *It is an advertisement. It's supposed to encourage people to want to come to a performance and watch amazing and daring feats!*

6. How does the artist who designed this poster want us to feel when we see it? Explain how you know using details and words from the picture. *We are supposed to be awestruck, curious, and amazed. The men look like they are very high in the air, and one almost looks like he is flying. Has the man on the left just launched the other into the air? Will the man on the right catch the one in the middle? What happens if he does not catch his brother? Is there a net? What other daring feats do these three perform? Where can I get a ticket to see this?*

Lesson 3.1

How Can Something Be More Than Itself?

The main purpose of the launch activity was to open a discussion about how it feels to learn. This might sound a little silly. Haven't students been learning in school for several years already? Do we really have to have this discussion? In the case of gifted learners, the answers may be surprising. When tasks are challenging, typical learners literally feel the challenge physically. I call this the little *icky* feeling inside our stomachs—that feeling when we're a bit frustrated and uncertain if we can meet a challenge. Some students experience this feeling every day, but often gifted learners do not. We want our gifted learners to understand that this feeling is not only natural, but also good; it signifies that they are being challenged to learn and grow.

In this lesson, you will help students build and analyze a metaphor for learning. In this case, students are going to create their own metaphor by connecting circus trapeze acrobats and learning. Metaphors are created when students combine a referent source (the image with the circus acrobats) with associated feelings and life experiences to form deeper meanings.

Materials

- » Handout 3.1: Wonderings: How Can Something Be More Than Itself?
- » Handout 3.1: Wonderings: How Can Something Be More Than Itself? Sample
- » Circus poster image (https://www.loc.gov/pictures/item/2007682627)

Estimated Time

- » 30 minutes

Procedure

Distribute Handout 3.1: Wonderings: How Can Something Be More Than Itself? A sample response for creating and understanding learning through metaphors is included on the page following the handout. Thoughtful and thorough students may want more room to write their responses and may become frustrated with the exercise. Consider using this handout as a visual aid to organize verbal group responses instead—allowing students to take notes in the blank spaces rather than write their responses in complete sentences. For each box in the graphic organizer, invite students to think quietly about their potential responses (for 30–60 seconds), share responses with a partner (2 minutes), and then participate in a discussion with the entire class (5 minutes). In this way, the collective energy of the classroom will come together to analyze and explain the complexities of a metaphorical comparison.

Encourage students to clarify their thinking and provide supporting examples. The sample answers for Handout 3.1 will help guide your discussion with students. You may choose to share key takeaways from the sample answers if students do not reach these discussion points on their own. Most importantly, invite several students to share their conclusions from the section at the bottom of the handout, which offers an area to capture the class's most important thoughts.

Now that students have experience analyzing a metaphor with the support of their classmates, they'll be more prepared to work through a metaphor analysis process on their own for future projects. Adapt this "Wonderings" tool again and again in your classroom. This powerful analysis tool works anytime students need to compare two things and discover what ideas link them together.

Handout 3.1

Wonderings: How Can Something Be More Than Itself?

Directions: Use this graphic organizer to describe and explain circus trapeze acrobats and learning. You will use your explanations to help make connections between the two.

How are circus trapeze acrobats similar to learning?
What do trapeze acrobats do? What is learning?
What is the purpose of trapeze acrobats? What is the purpose of learning?
How do people feel when watching acrobats? How do they feel when learning?
Have you ever watched acrobats? Tell us more. Describe a memory with learning that really sticks out in your mind.
Look at your descriptions above. What connections can you make between circus trapeze acrobats and learning?

Handout 3.1

Wonderings: How Can Something Be More Than Itself? Sample

Directions: Use this graphic organizer to describe and explain circus trapeze acrobats and learning. You will use your explanations to help make connections between the two.

How are circus trapeze acrobats similar to learning?
What do trapeze acrobats do? What is learning? *Flying through the air high above the ground, swinging on cables, catching and being caught.* *Doing things you've never done before or getting better and better at things you already knew about a little bit.*
What is the purpose of trapeze acrobats? What is the purpose of learning? *It entertains an audience, and it's challenging and engaging for the acrobats. It's an athletic feat.* *It's used to grow and get better. It's how we understand things we didn't used to understand or do things we've never done before.*
How do people feel when watching acrobats? How do they feel when learning? *It's thrilling and amazing. It feels very difficult. It can be scary. It seems daring. It's very satisfying when done right. It can give you a nervous feeling inside.* *It's very satisfying when you are successful. It can be frustrating, difficult, and even a little scary. It can give you an icky feeling inside.*
Have you ever watched acrobats? Tell us more. Describe a memory with learning that really sticks out in your mind. *No, but it reminds me of learning. The first time I went off the high diving board at the swimming pool. I was really nervous but felt proud when I succeeded.* *If I have to give a presentation, I'm really nervous about it, so I practice a lot to feel prepared and to be successful. It is difficult for me. Once I pretended like I was sick so I didn't have to do it.*
Look at your descriptions above. What connections can you make between circus trapeze acrobats and learning? *Trapeze acrobats get help from others to perform challenging and thrilling things . . . just like we get help from teachers to help us learn and grow and feel proud. Learning and trapeze flips aren't easy! They can both be scary. We really have to work at them to be successful.*

Lesson 3.2

Visualizing Resilience

Many of our students rely on visual avenues to create understanding, and analyzing a series of commercials in a thoughtful way may open insights for visual and spatial learners. In this activity, students will discuss the idea of greatness through Nike's "find your greatness" commercials—a series of vignettes displaying the talents and challenges of young athletes.

Materials

» Nike's "find your greatness" campaign commercials: Search online for individual videos or use the compilation found here: https://www.youtube.com/watch?v=WYP 9AGtLvRg.

Estimated Time

» 30 minutes

Procedure

Show students any or all of Nike's "find your greatness" campaign commercials. As of this printing, all of them are posted online. Before students watch the video(s), tell them to take note of the ones they enjoy, as you will be asking them to share their favorite Nike commercials in class discussion.

Pair-Share. After watching several commercials, have students share their favorite parts with a partner or small group. Ask a few students to share with the whole class. These videos demonstrate many components of a growth mindset—overcoming fear, trying hard, having fun with a challenge. Together, they are an inspiring review of previous discussions in Units 1 and 2:

- » What precious gift might you develop through persistence?
- » Does practice make perfect?
- » Is perfection even possible?
- » If you were featured in a commercial, which of your talents would be on display?
- » What is your greatness?

Class Discussion. In a whole-class discussion, have students consider the following questions:

- » These commercials show greatness, but they don't explain how a person arrived at greatness. How did these people arrive at greatness?
- » Do you think any of the people in the commercials had to have resilience to be great? In what way? Explain.
- » According to the commercials, what is greatness?
- » What does this quote from the Nike commercials mean to you?: "Greatness is not in one special person. Greatness is wherever somebody is trying to find it."

Key ideas from the commercials to discuss include:

- » Resilience means bouncing back.
- » Resilience means sometimes starting over and trying again.
- » Resilience means being willing to be unsuccessful because you will keep working until you achieve what you set out to do.

If possible, move to the next portion of the unit, Lesson 3.3: Bouncing Back, on a future day after students have had a chance to internalize the idea of resilience.

Lesson 3.3

Bouncing Back

In Lesson 3.3, you will present a visual metaphor for students. In a demonstration, you will examine a bouncy ball and then bounce the ball on the classroom floor in different ways and with different reactions. Students will make connections through a graphic organizer and through class discussion as they begin to create a metaphor that links resilience to bouncy balls.

Materials

- » Handout 3.3: Resilience
- » Handout 3.3: Resilience Sample
- » Bouncy ball (38 mm or about 1.5" diameter; I do not recommend any smaller than this)
- » Large, heavy textbook

Estimated Time

- » 20 minutes

Preparation

As the teacher, you will demonstrate each step with a bouncy ball. Make sure to practice each step in the Procedure section before class, especially Step 8, which requires some finesse.

Procedure

Demonstrate each of the following steps for students to see:
1. Hold a bouncy ball and ask students to describe what they see.
2. Drop the ball and ask for a description of what they see.
3. Smush the ball as best you can (or can't) under a big textbook. Describe what is observed.
4. Demonstrate both negative and positive self-talk by tossing the ball in the air and dropping it on purpose once or twice. Give up trying and speak your discouraged thoughts aloud. Sit down and act bored and purposeless. Resolve aloud to try again, sharing positive self-talk and encouraging words.
5. Now toss the ball in the air and catch it. Share your success with students, repeating aloud how you had been unsuccessful at first but then resolved to keep trying.
6. Toss the ball to a student, encourage them to catch it, and congratulate them if they do. Try again if necessary.
7. Ask the class what will happen when you toss the ball in front of you a couple of feet. Where will it go? Toss the ball so that it bounces away from you. Act disappointed that you've lost it.
8. Try Step 7 again. This time toss the ball in front of you a couple feet, but make sure to spin it toward you while doing so (here is where the practice in advance will pay off!). The spin makes the ball bounce back toward you. Ask students: *Wait a minute—how could this possibly happen?*

Note. This lesson can be easily expanded to cover Newton's third law of motion. See Lesson 3.6.

Follow-Up: Metaphor Activity

Using Handout 3.3: Resilience, challenge students to explain how playing with a bouncy ball is like resilience. This metaphor-building activity should be challenging. Have students work on the handout individually for 2 minutes, silently brainstorming. Then, give students a chance to share ideas with a partner. Finish the lesson by gathering the whole class to share ideas.

Discussion questions might include:
» If I said to you, "I really like your bounce," what would I mean?
» If I said, "I think you lost your bouncy ball," what would I mean?
» If I said, "This new math unit is going to take plenty of bouncy balls by the time we finish," what advice about the unit would I be giving you?
» If I said, "You're really going to have to *spin it* to complete this project," what would I mean?
» If I said, "I love it that you never seem to lose your bouncy ball," what compliment would I be giving?
» If I gave the advice, "Sometimes you need a good bouncy ball, and sometimes you don't," what would I be saying about learning new things?

NAME:_____ DATE:_____

Handout 3.3

Resilience

Directions: Think about your teacher's demonstration with the bouncy ball. Playing with a bouncy ball is like resilience in many ways! Think of three ways that playing with a bouncy ball is like resilience. Write your ideas in the boxes below.

<table>
<tr><td></td></tr>
</table>

<table>
<tr><td></td></tr>
</table>

<table>
<tr><td></td></tr>
</table>

NAME:_____ DATE: _____

Handout 3.3

Resilience Sample

Directions: Think about your teacher's demonstration with the bouncy ball. Playing with a bouncy ball is like resilience in many ways! Think of three ways that playing with a bouncy ball is like resilience. Write your ideas in the boxes below.

> *Everything is so much more fun if you don't lose it or let it get away from you!*

> *It's practically indestructible. It will always be there for you if you take care of it.*

> *It all comes bouncing back to you, especially if you put the right spin on it and treat it like a game.*

Social and Emotional Curriculum for Gifted Students, Grade 3 © Prufrock Press Inc.

The Class Data Challenge

In this lesson, it's the students' turn to try bouncing a ball so that it spins away from them and returns. In the process, they'll gather data and have fun doing it.

Materials

- » Handout 3.4: Bounce Back Challenge
- » Handout 3.4: Bounce Back Challenge Sample
- » Bouncy balls (one per student; bouncy balls purchased in bulk online could supply a classroom for 2 or more years)
- » Yardstick to measure distances and set up the challenge
- » Tape to mark the "challenge" lines

Estimated Time

- » 45 minutes

Preparation

Bouncy balls can be spun back to the person tossing them better when they bounce on carpet, so find an area in which the whole class can toss their bouncy balls in a practice session. Allow plenty of room to spread out. My school has a large, carpeted foyer that can accommodate an entire classroom. You might need to use the gym or the lunch room to find enough space at your school.

For this activity, students will stand in a line, shoulder to shoulder with a line taped at their feet and two other lines beyond it. It's best to set up tape lines in advance. Prepare two

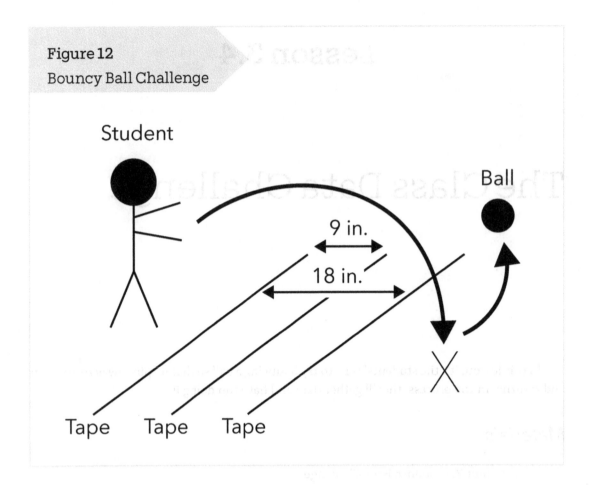

Figure 12
Bouncy Ball Challenge

additional lines of tape, one 9 inches past the first taped line and one 18 inches past. See Figure 12 for a diagram of how this will look.

While conducting this activity at my school, I found a "ready-made" line where the tile meets carpet in the foyer. I then taped lines 9 and 18 inches in front of the carpet-to-tile transition. You might be able to find something similar in your classroom or school to make preparations easier.

Procedure

Tell students: *Let's have a little more fun with the bouncy balls, gather data, think mathematically, and then extend our metaphor once again! This activity is going to take some extra bounce to complete.*

Distribute bouncy balls and allow students a few minutes to practice spinning the balls so they bounce back. This works best if the balls are spun/tossed only a couple feet in front of the tosser. In tossing and spinning the balls, students will quickly discover that spinning a ball so that it will bounce back to be caught is not as easy as it seems!

Present the challenge: Can students toss and spin the ball so that it crosses the 18-inch line and then reach out and catch the ball as it bounces back without crossing the line at their feet?

Encourage students to keep practicing—and be ready for things to get a bit crazy! While balls bounce all over the classroom, take advantage of the teachable moment. Ask students: *What if something seems a little too difficult? Do you just give up? Is it OK to adjust your goal to something still challenging but a little less "impossible"?*

Now point to the line of tape you've prepared that is closer to the starting line—9 inches away instead of 18 inches. Ask students: *Can you bounce the ball past the 9-inch line and catch it without stepping over the line at your feet?* With this change, students will be much more successful. It's time for another teachable moment: *Are you having more fun now? Why? Goals can be exciting if you don't give up and if they are challenging but not too easy. You can be successful if you are willing to be resilient.*

Once students have practiced for 5–10 additional minutes, ask the class to begin to gather data. Each student will toss the ball 10 times and count how many times they successfully tossed the ball across the 18- or 9-inch line (whichever you deem most appropriate) and then caught it without having to step across the line at their feet.

Note. While recording or presenting their data in this lesson, several students may not be honest about how successful they've been. If this occurs, this is a good opportunity to have a discussion with the whole class: *Why not just admit you didn't catch it 10 out of 10 times? Will you be more respected because you might have fibbed and seem like an expert ball bouncer, or because you were honest about how well you bounced the ball?*

Follow-Up: Math and Data

Once students have tallied the sum of successful tries, instruct them to complete Handout 3.4: Bounce Back Challenge. This should not become a contest. Students need not share their data with others; however, do encourage them to share their thoughts about growth mindset: *How is this activity related to a growth mindset? How does a growth mindset help a person meet challenges?*

Also have students consider the key math question (question #5 on Handout 3.4) and share their answers: *How can gathering data help us understand how difficult something is?* Sample answers are included on the page following the handout.

Handout 3.4

Bounce Back Challenge

Directions: Record your data and answer the following questions about your bouncy ball challenge.

1. Out of 10, how many times did you catch the ball without crossing the line?

2. Write the number above as a fraction.

3. According to the fraction above, if you tossed the ball 20 times instead of 10, how many times should you expect to catch it?

4. How does a growth mindset help you become better at tossing and catching?

5. How can gathering data help us understand how difficult something is?

Handout 3.4: Bounce Back Challenge, *continued*

Challenge

Warning: Entering this area may take resilience!

According to your fraction in Question 2, how many times should you expect to catch the ball if you tossed it 100 times?

How about 500 times?

150 times?

75 times?

Handout 3.4

Bounce Back Challenge Sample

Directions: Record your data and answer the following questions about your bouncy ball challenge.

1. Out of 10, how many times did you catch the ball without crossing the line?

   4 times

2. Write the number above as a fraction.

   $\frac{4}{10}$

3. According to the fraction above, if you tossed the ball 20 times instead of 10, how many times should you expect to catch it?

   4 x 2 = 8
   8 times

4. How does a growth mindset help you become better at tossing and catching?

   If you keep trying and practicing and stay positive, you will get better.

5. How can gathering data help us understand how difficult something is?

   We can see how successful many people are. Lower fractions mean the task is more difficult.

Social and Emotional Curriculum for Gifted Students, Grade 3 © Prufrock Press Inc.

Handout 3.4: Bounce Back Challenge Sample, *continued*

Challenge

Warning: Entering this area may take resilience!

According to your fraction in Question 2, how many times should you expect to catch the ball if you tossed it 100 times?

40

How about 500 times?

200

150 times?

60

75 times?

30

Empowering Words of Encouragement

Students will write words of encouragement for themselves and their classmates on the bouncy balls.

Materials

- » Handout 3.5: Empowering Words of Encouragement
- » Bouncy balls (one per student—to write on and keep)
- » Permanent markers

Estimated Time

- » 20 minutes

Procedure

After completing the tossing and spinning challenge in the previous lesson, students will see that, wow, that challenge was a challenge indeed! After this potentially frustrating challenge, now is the time to help your students understand that there are times in everyone's life when it's necessary to gather oneself together, regroup, and seek encouragement.

Using Handout 3.5: Empowering Words of Encouragement, have students brainstorm words of encouragement for someone who may need them. Talk about a time when you felt discouraged but were able to be successful in the end. What sort of encouragement did you get from others? What helped you bounce back? What thoughts helped you get back on track again?

Figure 13
Bouncy Ball Messages

When students have generated encouraging words using Handout 3.4, they should write these words with a permanent marker on a bouncy ball (see Figure 13), and—surprise!—give it to themselves as a reminder to stay positive.

It's the small things in life that are satisfying sometimes. Your students will be thrilled that they get to keep the bouncy balls.

Handout 3.5

Empowering Words of Encouragement

Directions: Everyone needs a little encouragement from time to time. Use this activity sheet to brainstorm words of encouragement for someone who may be having a bad day or is getting down on themselves. Maybe that person is fearful or is just plain worn out. What words could you share to encourage that person to be resilient—to bounce back—and to gather themselves back up again and give it another try?

Brainstorm ideas in the following circles. Then, using a permanent marker, write your best idea for encouragement on your bouncy ball.

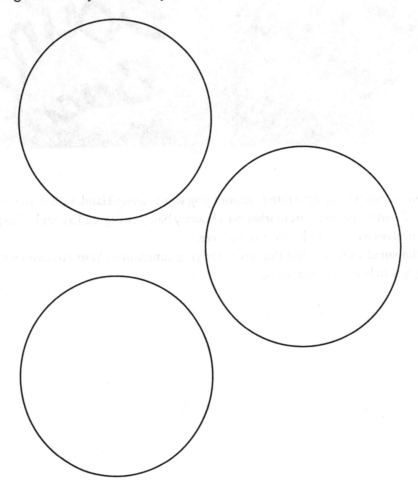

< UNIT 3: BOUNCING BACK >

Social and Emotional Curriculum for Gifted Students, Grade 3 © Prufrock Press Inc.

Action and Reaction Extension

This lesson works well for a gifted pull-out group extension. I would advise against treating it as a comprehensive study—it is more like an introduction to concepts in math and science that students will learn in more detail in future grades.

Consider the exposure to new math concepts for third graders in this extension, which:

» shows that a meter stick consists of 100 centimeters and shows the relationship between the number of centimeters and decimals,

» teaches students how to read a meter stick (as 1 m, 0.75 m, 0.50 m, 0.25 m, etc.),

» helps explain to students that decimals are fractions (e.g., What fraction is 0.5?),

» explains how a meter is easy to convert into a decimal (to the nearest 100th) made up of meters and centimeters,

» explains how to convert a decimal to a percentage and introduces what a percentage represents, and

» shows how to use a calculator to divide numbers, such as 0.75.

Keep in mind that students are not expected to master these math concepts. Gifted and talented students should respond well and, depending on their talent area, will "get" most of it. If they're confused, then all the better! Here lies another opportunity to emphasize growth mindset. Remind your gifted learners that not only is it OK to be a bit frustrated, but also it's the heart of learning.

Materials

» Handout 3.6: The Way the Ball Bounces
» Handout 3.6: The Way the Ball Bounces Sample
» Experiment materials (per pair of students):
  » Meter stick

69

» Bouncy ball
» Calculator
» Tape

» Other types of balls, like baseballs or golf balls (optional)

Estimated Time

» 60 minutes

Procedure

Tell students: *Now we will study action/reaction in an experiment, gather data, and assign mathematical values to our experiment results.*

Tape a meter stick vertically to a wall so that 0 centimeters rests against the floor. Begin a discussion about how a meter stick is made up of 100 centimeters and how this can apply to decimals. Explain to students that 75 centimeters, for example, can be read as 0.75 meters. Ask: *What decimal value of a meter is 50 centimeters? What about 33 centimeters?*

Distribute Handout 3.6: The Way the Ball Bounces. Have students work in pairs to complete it. Student pairs should drop their bouncy ball from the height indicated in the left column and observe how high the ball bounces. It will take several drops from each height in order to reach consensus about how high the ball bounces back. This is somewhat imprecise; however, the observation process will serve students' understanding of physics concepts well. Students should record results on the chart.

Then, students will use a calculator to complete the second column of the chart in Handout 3.6. Show students how to do this. Third graders may not have used calculators very often. This will be a lesson in and of itself.

Show students how to convert a decimal to a percentage, and explain what percentages mean. In my state, work with percentages doesn't appear until the sixth- and seventh-grade standards. Remember, this is an introduction, although most gifted students identified for mathematical ability will understand percentages very quickly and intuitively.

While working with decimals, students should also practice reading them correctly. For example, 0.25 meters = "twenty-five one-hundredths meters." Gifted students will make connections with fractions in this way as well.

Just for Fun. Outside or in the gym, find a soccer ball, basketball, or dodgeball. Place a bouncy ball on top of the larger ball. Drop them together in this way, and watch what happens. Be careful and stay back after you bounce the balls together. The bouncy ball will be catapulted high and fast as it bounces off the larger ball. Don't make the mistake of trying this inside your classroom like I did. I was lucky I didn't break a ceiling tile or light fixture!

Follow-Up: Discussion

Ask students to share their observations. Can students reach consensus on important understandings? Questions and possible answers might include the following:

» If every action has an equal and opposite reaction, why doesn't the ball bounce back as high as it was dropped? *Some of the energy from the falling ball is absorbed into the ball when it hits the floor, and some of the energy is released in the sound waves produced after the ball hits the floor.*

» Would different sorts of balls give us different results? *Quite possibly—depending on the ball's elasticity.*

» Will a ball ever bounce back higher than it was dropped? *Not unless force is added. If you throw the ball toward the floor, it will bounce back higher. Remember, every action has an equal and opposite reaction.*

If there's time, students can test different balls' elasticity. A golf ball is quite elastic. It bounces very high compared to, say, a baseball dropped from the same height, which is not nearly as elastic as a golf ball. Will the elasticity have an effect other "bounce-back" percentage? Encourage students who finish the lesson quickly to try this out.

Handout 3.6

The Way the Ball Bounces

Directions: Drop the ball from the heights listed in the left column. Pay close attention to details. Complete the chart for each height listed using a calculator.

Drop Height	Bounce-Back Height	Bounce-Back Height Divided by Drop Height	Converted to Percentage
1.0 m			
0.75 m			
0.5 m			
0.25 m			

Scientist Notes and Observations: What did you observe? What patterns or trends do you notice?

For every action, there is an equal and opposite reaction.

Handout 3.6

The Way the Ball Bounces Sample

Directions: Drop the ball from the heights listed in the left column. Pay close attention to details. Complete the chart for each height listed using a calculator.

Drop Height	Bounce-Back Height	Bounce-Back Height Divided by Drop Height	Converted to Percentage
1.0 m	0.86 m	0.86 m	86%
0.75 m	0.66 m	0.88 m	88%
0.5 m	0.45 m	0.9 m	90%
0.25 m	0.22 m	0.88 m	88%

Scientist Notes and Observations: What did you observe? What patterns or trends do you notice?

Each time, I have observed a gap between the drop height and the bounce-back height. The ball never bounces back as high as it was dropped. The ball, no matter at what height it begins its drop, bounces back at about 88% of the original height it is dropped from each time.

For every action, there is an equal and opposite reaction.

Unit 4

SUITCASES AND CIRCLES OF HOPE

Identity

Background

In this unit, students imagine what precious possessions they would pack into their scant luggage as an Ellis Island immigrant. They then create representations of these items and fill a suitcase with these items. In preparation for the activities, students examine two primary source photos and make inferences using the details in the photos. In an exhibition of learning, students display their suitcase and items in a gallery walk—an excellent activity for an open house or during parent-teacher conferences. Finally, students imagine their best futures, which are also displayed in a gallery walk.

The hands-on nature of this lesson is intended to encourage high engagement and creative opportunities for students, build empathy and understanding, and encourage guided higher order thinking skills. All learners are 21st-century learners—who communicate and collaborate, engage in critical thinking, and creatively meet the needs of an ever-expanding global community.

This unit works wonderfully as a part of a larger exploration on immigration or the Ellis Island and Angel Island periods in U.S. history. With that in mind, this is not a detailed history lesson; instead, the purpose of this unit is to lay important emotional and cultural groundwork for history lessons on immigration and to invite students into an accepting and

75

understanding mindset. Although this lesson takes students deeper into the imagined life of an immigrant, you may need to fill in gaps in students' knowledge about Ellis Island or Angel Island.

Unit Objectives

Students will:
» identify the people, things, talents, and ideas that are most important in their lives; and
» express their hopes for the future.

NAGC Learning and Development Standards

1.1. Self-Understanding. Students with gifts and talents recognize their interests, strengths, and needs in cognitive, creative, social, emotional, and psychological areas.

1.2. Self-Understanding. Students with gifts and talents demonstrate understanding of how they learn and recognize the influences of their identities, cultures, beliefs, traditions, and values on their learning and behavior.

1.3. Self-Understanding. Students with gifts and talents demonstrate understanding of and respect for similarities and differences between themselves and their cognitive and chronological peer groups and others in the general population.

Themes and Skills Addressed

Social-Emotional Theme
» Identity

Academic Skills
» Inferences
» Collaborative discussion
» Metaphor analysis
» Metaphor creation
» Graphic design
» Building and engineering

Launch

Share your favorite picture book about immigration with your students. Two of my favorites are *When Jessie Came Across the Sea* by Amy Hest, and *Coming to America: The Story of Immigration* by Betsy Maestro. Both books serve as an excellent reference for the historical period, places, and emotions connected with Ellis Island. Louise Peacock's *At Ellis Island: A*

History in Many Voices provides both strong emotional background as well as historical details. It's a much longer read-aloud. In the past, I have read aloud parts of it and then invited students to read the book in its entirety on their own.

Discuss the following:

» What feelings do the illustrations communicate? Point to specific pictures to support your ideas.

» Have you ever moved to a new home or a new school? Did you have worries about what would happen in the new place? How did you feel in the days before you left and during your move? How did you feel when you first came to the new place?

» What would have been going through your mind as an immigrant on the journey to America?

Lesson 4.1

Primary Source Photo Analysis

In this lesson, students examine primary source photos from Ellis Island and think critically about the images, making inferences and drawing conclusions in a discussion.

Materials

» Handout 4.1: Image Response Form
» Handout 4.1: Image Response Form Sample
» Photos from the Library of Congress National Archives
  » Landing at Ellis Island (https://www.loc.gov/pictures/item/97501086)
  » Immigrants carrying luggage, Ellis Island, New York (https://www.loc.gov/pictures/item/2014683246)

Estimated Time

» 20 minutes

Procedure

With the whole class, examine the Ellis Island photos on Handout 4.1: Image Response Form. You may distribute the handout to students and/or display the photos for all students to see. Explain visual analysis to students: *If we are analyzing written text, we first have to read the words. Similarly, in a visual analysis, we first have to "read" the details of the photo.*

Begin by inviting students to point out details in the photos, like suitcases, clothing, buildings, boats, walkways, and what is seen in the background. Invite students to look closely—to describe details of a facial expression or in an article of clothing. Invite them to ask questions and to wonder. Do not allow students to make inferences yet. Gifted students are often impatient with analysis because their minds make connections so quickly. They want to jump directly to inferences or make conclusions. Try not to let them do this. In this way, help students gather important observations, which they will use for inferences and more complex thinking activities later.

Have students finish responding to the questions on Handout 4.1. Students may work together in groups, in partners, or individually, depending upon their background and experience. Sample answers are included on the page following the handout.

Handout 4.1

Image Response Form

Directions: Consider the images and answer the questions that follow.

"Landing at Ellis Island" as illustrated in "Quarantine Sketches," 1902, p. 25, from The Maltine Company. United States Library of Congress Prints and Photographs Division. https://www.loc.gov/pictures/item/97501086

1. What emotions or mood do you see expressed in this photo? Point out specific details to support your response.

2. These immigrants have just traveled for thousands of miles, across an ocean, to a country to begin a new life; however, all of their possessions can be carried with them in a couple of suitcases and satchels. Infer what this tells us about them. Explain.

Handout 4.1: Image Response Form, *continued*

"Immigrants Carrying Luggage," circa 1910, The Bain News Service. United States Library of Congress Prints and Photographs Division. https://www.loc.gov/pictures/item/2014683246

3. Where do you think this photo was taken? Use inferences and details from the photo to explain your answer.

4. Are all of the people in the photo immigrants? Support your answer with inferences and details from the photo.

NAME:_____ DATE: _____

Handout 4.1

Image Response Form Sample

Directions: Consider the images and answer the questions that follow.

"Landing at Ellis Island" as illustrated in "Quarantine Sketches," 1902, p. 25, from The Maltine Company. United States Library of Congress Prints and Photographs Division. https://www.loc.gov/pictures/item/97501086

1. What emotions or mood do you see expressed in this photo? Point out specific details to support your response.

   I see emotions of wonder, a mood of hope despite the drab clothing and surroundings, and an eagerness as well. The wide eyes on so many show a wonderment of their new surroundings. They look up and forward, their bodies leaning toward their destination. This shows a hope and an eager feeling that comes with starting something new—even when there is uncertainty of what may come.

2. These immigrants have just traveled for thousands of miles, across an ocean, to a country to begin a new life; however, all of their possessions can be carried with them in a couple of suitcases and satchels. Infer what this tells us about them. Explain.

   They probably had few possessions to begin with, and they could only take so much with them. They were probably looking for a better life. They must have put only the most important items into their suitcases and satchels. They were taking a big chance by leaving almost everything behind. They must have been scared but full of hope, too.

Handout 4.1: Image Response Form Sample, *continued*

"Immigrants Carrying Luggage," circa 1910, The Bain News Service. United States Library of Congress Prints and Photographs Division. https://www.loc.gov/pictures/item/2014683246

3. Where do you think this photo was taken? Use inferences and details from the photo to explain your answer.

    First, it says "Ellis Island" at the top. It is probably taken on docks where ships arrived with immigrants from Europe. I notice the wooden planks of a dock and a cart that might be used to unload ships or haul around freight. It looks like ocean in the background because it is wide open. They must have arrived not too long before the picture was taken because they are still carrying luggage.

4. Are all of the people in the photo immigrants? Support your answer with inferences and details from the photo.

    The woman and the boy closest may not be immigrants. They are dressed in brighter shades—less drab and fancier—than the others. They look like they are well off financially, whereas a recent immigrant would not likely be. They are not carrying any suitcases. The woman is turning away with her hands on her hip like she is "stand-offish" and "better" than the others. The boy is looking toward the immigrants, like "Who are those people?" while his mom is sort of shielding him.

Handout 4.1: Image Response Form Sample

Lesson 4.2

What Items Will You Take?

In this lesson, students imagine they are about to embark on the journey of an immigrant, yet they have room for only three personal items (aside from essentials like clothing) in their suitcases. Students must choose three small items representing the people most supportive of them and their talents most dear.

Materials

»   Handout 4.2: Suitcase Brainstorming Sheet
»   Handout 4.2: Filling Your Suitcase
»   Handout 4.2: Filling Your Suitcase Sample

Estimated Time

»   30–40 minutes

Procedure

Review and Background. As an additional background and a mindset activity, visit the Ellis Island website (https://nps.gov/elis/index.htm) together as a class to view images of immigrants as they first arrived in America. Alternatively, search the web for images from Angel Island as well. Students will see photographs of immigrants with battered suitcases in tow. Invite students to imagine taking part in the processing experience at one of the grand immigration processing centers—being catalogued, tagged, labelled, and evaluated as they make their way into a land where their hopes lie. Clarify questions students might have and fill in gaps in knowledge around the processing that occurred at Ellis and Angel Islands. It may also be useful to refer back to the picture books that were shared in the launch activity.

Tell students: *There was only so much a person could carry. Necessities like clothing filled the suitcases, but what other items—items special and dear to their owners—were packed inside those suitcases?*

Ask students to imagine they are about to embark on the journey of an immigrant. Depending on the demographics of your own classroom, you may want to substitute current-day immigrants for those who arrived at Ellis and Angel Islands about 100 years ago. Ask students to imagine they have just enough room to pack three items, which represent people or things most dear to them. These items have to be small. What will they be?

Brainstorming and Planning. Have students complete Handout 4.2: Suitcase Brainstorming Sheet to help generate ideas. Encourage patience with this process. Gifted students are all too eager to race ahead. Here is an opportunity to slow down and reflect upon people, things, and ideas that are important to them.

After completing the brainstorming activity, students should complete Handout 4.2: Filling Your Suitcase for the three items they've chosen to bring with them. Tell students: *Now that you have finished brainstorming, it's time to select three items to take along with you on your journey. Complete the graphic organizer to explain why you've chosen these items.*

Students must create metaphors to represent people, pets, or ideas, as these things cannot be packed inside a suitcase. In this way, the students' planning process requires deeper critical and representational thinking. Additionally, students will plan to bring items from these three categories:

» **An ability or idea that helps them find success in their lives:** Gifted programming should focus decidedly on a student's abilities rather than on their deficits. In this spirit, students will brainstorm ideas or qualities that they might rely upon each day. For example, one student cited making connections as an important quality: "I feel happier because of the people I know at school and the teachers and coaches who have been guides in my life," she said. She eventually represented "making connections" with a keychain.

» **Something or someone who provides comfort:** As intense individuals who may experience life more vividly than others, gifted learners can be prone to anxiety. Finding comfort in beliefs, people, or things that provide safe places—both physically and emotionally—is one way of coping with stress. One student chose their bookshelf in their bedroom as a comforting part of their life: "I can go anywhere I want when I open a book. I can find peace if I want it. I can find thrills and adventure, too!" A bookshelf is obviously much too large and heavy for a suitcase, so the student chose to represent her bookshelf with a bookmark listing her favorite books.

» **Free choice:** Students may choose any number of items as the free choice, and as teachers, we are reminded that gifted kids are kids, after all, even though they may think like adults. Game consoles, smartphones, and sports equipment are common choices. Even though we may want our students to choose deeply meaningful and symbolic items (like a smooth stone that reminds them of the outing they took to the mountains with their beloved family one spring day), students can't go wrong as long as they choose an item dear to them.

Make sure to save students' completed copies of Handout 4.2: Filling Your Suitcase. These will come in handy as students prepare for their gallery walk display later on in the unit. Sample answers may be found on the page following the handout.

Handout 4.2

Suitcase Brainstorming Sheet

Directions: Complete the following questions to help you brainstorm what items you might want to pack in your suitcase.

1. Who are you? Yes, your name, but really, who *are* you?

2. What do you like to do with friends?

3. Who are the people most important to you?

4. When you spend time alone, what do you do?

5. What afterschool sports or activities do you participate in?

6. Where is the place you feel most at home?

UNIT 4: SUITCASES AND CIRCLES OF HOPE

Handout 4.2: Suitcase Brainstorming Sheet, *continued*

7. What is something you know a lot about?

8. What are the best gifts you've ever received that didn't cost any money?

9. Who is the most interesting person you know?

10. Whom do you admire?

11. What do you value most?

12. What is one item you own that seems to say, "This is who I am"?

Social and Emotional Curriculum for Gifted Students, Grade 3 © Prufrock Press Inc.

Handout 4.2

Filling Your Suitcase

Directions: You must select three items that represent people or things that are special to you. Because you can only bring small items, you may have to substitute items that *represent* the people or things. You can't, for example, bring your dog—but you can bring her dog tag, which will remind you of how special she is to you.

Item	Why It's Special to You	How It Will Be Represented
Item 1: An ability or idea that will help you find success in your life.		
Item 2: Someone or something that will give you comfort in times of trouble.		
Item 3: Free choice.		

Handout 4.2

Filling Your Suitcase Sample

Directions: You must select three items that represent people or things that are special to you. Because you can only bring small items, you may have to substitute items that *represent* the people or things. You can't, for example, bring your dog–but you can bring her dog tag, which will remind you of how special she is to you.

Item	Why It's Special to You	How It Will Be Represented
Item 1: An ability or idea that will help you find success in your life. *Creativity, ideas, and artwork*	*I love to create art and write stories, and I really like to tie them together with comics. I will fill my time with ideas, artwork, and stories. I can use my creative talents in unlimited ways–from figuring out how to survive, to learning a new language, to finding a job.*	*Notebook*
Item 2: Someone or something that will give you comfort in times of trouble. *Connections with people I love*	*I need to stay in contact with everyone I love. I will want to talk to them, see them, and know about what is going on in their lives. I can do this best with a smartphone because it has video chat and ways to share pictures. Bonus: I can have a world of information at my fingertips.*	*Smartphone*
Item 3: Free choice. *Samie the beagle*	*My dog Samie. I can't imagine not having one of my best buddies along with me. She sleeps in my bed every night and howls every day when I come home from school.*	*Dog tags*

< UNIT 4: SUITCASES AND CIRCLES OF HOPE >

Social and Emotional Curriculum for Gifted Students, Grade 3 © Prufrock Press Inc.

Lesson 4.3

Building Suitcases and Crafting Items

Once students have planned the three items they will place in their suitcase (see Lesson 4.2), it's time to construct the suitcases and craft the items to go inside.

Materials

- » Construction paper
- » Glue, tape, and scissors
- » Cardboard panels and small boxes (one per student)
- » Various craft items or junk drawer items (e.g., pipe cleaners, craft sticks, string, beads, tissue paper, small plastic parts, small plastic animals or action figures, small wooden wheels, keyrings, small electronic parts)
- » Cardstock (optional)
- » Floral shears, pliers, or wire cutters (optional, for cutting craft sticks)
- » Low-temperature hot glue (optional)
- » Classroom drafting kits (optional)

Estimated Time

- » 40–60 minutes

Procedure

Present students with the materials they will need to create their suitcases and items (see Materials section). Shoeboxes work great for suitcases, and small boxes of many types are handy for creating three-dimensional objects. Some students will lovingly create these

Figure 14
Example Shoebox Suitcase

items—and for a good reason, as these items often represent their strongest emotions. Be generous about the time necessary for this portion of the unit. Students with a creative flair may want to work past one whole class session or more than one hour. It is, however, time well spent. As students create physical representations, they consciously and unconsciously reflect upon the ideas, people, and skills these items represent, thereby internalizing important understandings.

A shoebox can be transformed into a vintage suitcase with construction paper and glue, and it makes for a good place to store the items a student chooses. See Figure 14 for an example of a suitcase shoebox. Figure 15 shows the dog tags, cell phone, and notebook from the sample responses in Lesson 4.2 (see Handout 4.2: Filling Your Suitcase Sample).

Tips on Making a Suitcase
» Tissue boxes and shoe boxes work well.
» Make the suitcase look like an antique with some brown and black markers or strips of construction paper.
» Tie or glue string to the suitcase to make it look like the suitcase is falling apart.
» Several of my students have enjoyed making a latch to hold the suitcase shut. One way to create a latch is to hot glue a small loop of pipe cleaner or string on the top of the suitcase. Glue a small bead on the other side of the suitcase, which the pipe cleaner or string will wrap around.

Figure 15
Example Suitcase Items

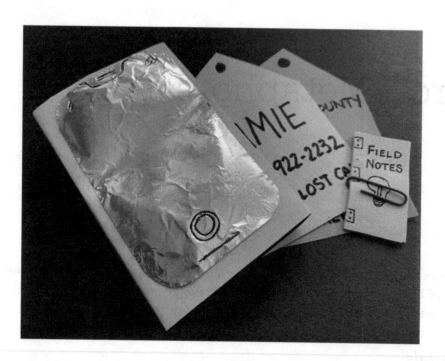

Tips on Crafting the Items for the Suitcase

» Three-dimensional items display much better than others. One way to make 3-D items is to draw a flat, one-dimensional picture of the item, cut it out, and trace it—making a copy. Tape the edges of these two copies together and stuff them with tissue paper.

» Beads, pipe cleaners, and craft sticks go miles and miles for craft projects. An easy way to cut craft sticks is with a pair of floral shears, pliers, or wire cutters. Don't use scissors—they'll break.

» Notecards or small pieces of cardboard can be cut and taped together to make just about any 3-D item.

» Small wooden wheels make a great supplement to craft sticks. When combined with dowels, they make a wheel and axle assembly that can be intriguing to young engineers.

» Low-temperature hot glue will expand the possibilities of crafting immensely. It's cheap and safe, too.

» Save small boxes, packaging, and broken toys. You never know when they might become an important piece of a project.

Lesson 4.4

Circle Metaphors

Before beginning the Circles of Hope activity, the class will take a deeper dive into the symbol of a circle. Some objects or words have become powerful symbols. A circle is one of those powerfully symbolic objects, and *portal* is a powerfully symbolic word.

Materials

» Handout 4.4: Wonderings: What Is a Circle?
» Handout 4.4: Wonderings: What Is a Circle? Sample
» Image of the Olympic rings

Estimated Time

» 20 minutes

Procedure

Because we're never too far from an Olympic year, use the well-known symbol of the Olympic rings to begin examining the symbol and metaphor of a circle. Show students an image of the Olympic rings. Ask them if they know what the Olympic rings stand for. Students should understand that the five rings signify the five regions of the world that originally came together for the Olympic Games. The "coming together" in unity during the games follows logically. But ask students: *Why a circle or rings? Why are circles a good metaphor for the Olympics?*

Guide students in their thinking to understand that circles might stand for perfection, strength, unity, and safety.

94

Distribute Handout 4.4: Wonderings: What Is a Circle? Students will use the handout to extend their thoughts about how a circle can be more than a circle. Sample answers may be found on the page following the handout.

NAME:_____ DATE:_____

Handout 4.4
Wonderings: What Is a Circle?

Directions: How can something be more than the thing itself? Complete this sheet with your wonderings about circles.

What is a circle? Write or draw what you think.

How is a circle used? What is its purpose?

Social and Emotional Curriculum for Gifted Students, Grade 3 © Prufrock Press Inc.

Handout 4.4: Wonderings: What Is a Circle? *continued*

How do people feel about circles?

What connections can you make between circles and your own life?

I'm beginning to think a circle is more than it seems . . .

NAME:_____ DATE:_____

Handout 4.4

Wonderings: What Is a Circle? Sample

Directions: How can something be more than the thing itself? Complete this sheet with your wonderings about circles.

What is a circle? Write or draw what you think.

It is perfectly round with infinite lines of symmetry. Follow any point in any direction on its path, and you will always return to where you began. It encloses an empty space inside.

How is a circle used? What is its purpose?

It is used in geometry and for many different designs. It is used as decoration. It is used for building blocks of cylinders in engineering. It brings people together when we sit in a circle so we can be good listeners.

Handout 4.4: Wonderings: What Is a Circle? Sample, *continued*

How do people feel about circles?

I think people usually like the look of a circle. A circle can make your feel together or in the safety of others. A circle can make you feel included. A circle can help you feel like something special is kept safely inside. Teams make a huddle of them.

What connections can you make between circles and your own life?

It makes me think of the times in class when we sit in a circle in the morning when everyone reports on good things that have happened to them and when we offer encouragement and compliments to classmates.

I'm beginning to think a circle is more than it seems... *Circles are about perfection and togetherness. Circles can make us feel secure, safe, and understood. They are strong—like being used for engineering and design.*

Handout 4.4 World Hinge: What Is a Circle? Sample, continued

Lesson 4.5

Circles of Hope

In this lesson, students imagine traveling in a ship to America and looking out a portal—imagining the hopes and dreams inside their heads while sailing to a new country. They look out of the ship's portal, and that portal is their "circle of hope." With what hopes and dreams will they fill their circle of hope?

Materials

- » Handout 4.5: A Circle of Hope
- » Handout 4.5: A Circle of Hope Sample
- » Colored pencils or markers

Estimated Time

- » 30 minutes

Procedure

Lead a discussion on portals: *What is a portal?* Students should understand that a portal can be both a window and an opening to another place. Portals are also the circular windows on ships. One hundred years ago and more, most immigrants to the United States arrived on ships. Depending on the age and background knowledge of your students, help them understand immigration, travel by ships, and the conditions under which most immigrants traveled to the United States. Once again, you may choose to reexamine, along with students, the picture books used to open this unit. Ask students: *How were the portals on these steamships both a window and an opening that led to a different place?*

Figure 16
Freedom Portal

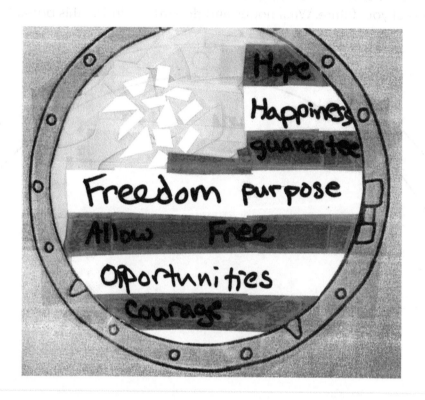

Now imagine a more timely scenario: Instead of 19th- or early 20th-century immigrants watching from a steamship's portal, our students are 21st-century immigrants soaring through outer space in a spaceship that will take them to a newly colonized planet. Each immigrant to this new colony will come with hopes and dreams to make a happy and fulfilling life for themselves in an ideal place, a cherished home for all people who arrive.

Present this scenario to students and have them complete Handout 4.5: A Circle of Hope. They will place their circles of hope in a gallery walk exhibition along with the suitcases and items they created in Lesson 4.3.

One of my students asked me (pointing at the portal), "How do I put *freedom* in there?"

"Well," I asked. "How *do* you? I am curious to see your solution!" With one simple question she helped solidify the metaphorical power of this lesson. See Figure 16 for her solution.

Handout 4.5

A Circle of Hope

Directions: On the spaceship soaring toward a new life, you look out of a round portal, hopefully dreaming of your future. What hopes and dreams live inside this portal?

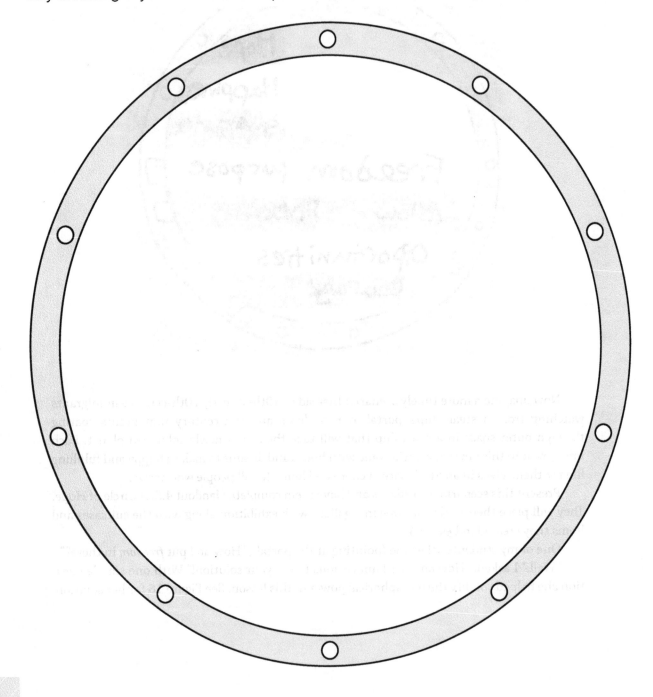

Handout 4.5

A Circle of Hope Sample

Directions: On the spaceship soaring toward a new life, you look out of a round portal, hopefully dreaming of your future. What hopes and dreams live inside this portal?

Gallery Walk

Students will share their Circles of Hope, their suitcases, and the items inside the suitcases in a gallery walk.

Materials

- » Handout 4.2: Filling Your Suitcase
- » Handout 4.5: A Circle of Hope
- » Handout 4.6: Gallery Walk Feedback Forms
- » 5" x 8" notecards (one per student)

Estimated Time

- » 30–60 minutes, depending on the size of the class

Procedure

Students will share their Circles of Hope, their suitcases, and the items inside the suitcases in a gallery walk. For the gallery walk, desks may be arranged to make a clearer walkway for the gallery's viewers. Hallways also work well—lining both sides of the hallway outside of a classroom with the students' displays. The Circles of Hope might be mounted on a construction paper matte. Students will arrange their suitcase items for easy viewing on desktops. Have students fold the large notecards so they become small informational placards for the suitcase items. Each informational placard should include a brief description of the item, what it represents if it is a metaphor, and information about why the item is important. This information can be transcribed from Handout 4.2: Filling Your Suitcase.

Prepare for the gallery walk by splitting the class into two groups. One group will stand beside their gallery display and answer questions, and the other group will circulate around the gallery as viewers. Then, the groups can switch roles so that all students are able to present their creations. This is an excellent informal public speaking activity. Model the way students might greet viewers and invite them to take a closer look at the items:

> "Hello, my name is _____. Thank you for viewing the items in my suitcase. As you look through the items, please let me know if you have any questions. I'll be glad to explain why they are important to me."

Finally, students should complete the first page of Handout 4.6: Gallery Walk Feedback Forms for each of their classmates, providing feedback before their parents or other classes are invited to attend the gallery walk.

If this activity is part of an open house or if other classrooms are invited to participate in the gallery walk, urge viewers to complete the second page of Handout 4.6: Gallery Walk Feedback Forms. Part of the intention of these forms is to illustrate connections between the viewers and the students, and part of the intention is to urge reflection for all participants.

Handout 4.6

Gallery Walk Feedback Forms

Teacher directions: Use the following forms for the gallery walk. The forms on the first page may be used by students in your class. The forms on the second page may be used by other classes or parents who view the gallery walk.

Class Feedback Form

What item would you add to this suitcase to complement the other items? Why?

What about this presentation or display impresses you?

What connections can you draw between this Circle of Hope and your own?

One question a viewer might ask about the display:

Class Feedback Form

What item would you add to this suitcase to complement the other items? Why?

What about this presentation or display impresses you?

What connections can you draw between this Circle of Hope and your own?

One question a viewer might ask about the display:

Guest Feedback Form

Which item might you also bring with you if you had to fill your own suitcase?

Which item was crafted in an interesting or skillful way?

If you had to make your own Circle of Hope, what would be inside?

Other comments:

Guest Feedback Form

Which item might you also bring with you if you had to fill your own suitcase?

Which item was crafted in an interesting or skillful way?

If you had to make your own Circle of Hope, what would be inside?

Other comments:

Feature Profile Test Extension

The Feature Profile Test was a wooden block puzzle test administered to Ellis Island immigrants because typical IQ tests involved language translation issues. The Feature Profile Test became an instant nonverbal IQ assessment. It was made from wooden blocks that—if placed in the proper order—formed the profile of a human face. According to the *Smithsonian* magazine, this test was used at Ellis Island in the early 1900s to keep out "feeble-minded" immigrants (Cohen, 2017, para. 2). The idea was that if an immigrant could not assemble the puzzle properly, then this person could not contribute to a better class of American citizenry.

In this lesson, students will complete their own puzzles and discuss the Feature Profile Test. For more information about the test, listen to this story on NPR: https://www.npr.org/2017/05/17/528813842/this-simple-puzzle-test-sealed-the-fate-of-immigrants-at-ellis-island.

Materials

- » Handout 4.7: Feature Profile Puzzle Template
- » Cardstock or heavy paper

Estimated Time

- » 20–30 minutes

Preparation

Create your own Feature Profile Test using the template on Handout 4.7: Feature Profile Puzzle Template. Before beginning the lesson, cut out the puzzle shapes included on the handout. In the past, I have constructed four or five puzzles and laminated the pieces so that I may reuse them in the future.

Procedure

Without much introduction, lay the puzzles out on several desktops and invite students to complete the puzzles in small groups. Invariably, students will exclaim at how easy the puzzles are, but that's actually part of the point and preparation for the discussion.

Share information and historical background about the Feature Profile Test with students. Then, as a class, discuss the following questions:

» Is the Feature Profile Test a more fair IQ test than a test based on language?
» Why did early 1900s immigration officials want to test for "feeble-mindedness"?
» Is it fair to deny entry to immigrants based on their intelligence?
» What are some reasons an immigrant might not have done well on the test?
» Is it important to test people for intelligence?

Handout 4.7

Feature Profile Puzzle Template

Teacher directions: Use this template to create a paper version of the Feature Profile Test. Cut out the shapes on the dashed lines. Then, use cardstock/heavy paper or laminate the pieces so that the puzzle may be used again and again.

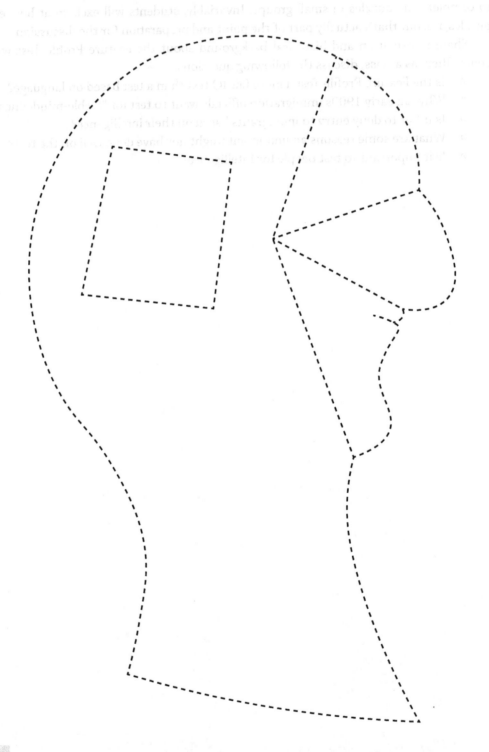

Social and Emotional Curriculum for Gifted Students, Grade 3 © Prufrock Press Inc.

UNIT 5

WHAT COMES FROM THE HEART

Empathy and Compassion

Background

Start the school year or the second semester with a powerful metaphor about what gifts we bring to the world—including an important example about using abilities and talents for academic achievement. Use this social-emotional unit as a pathway to thinking about gifted learners and achievement or any other important social-emotional understanding. Need a pathway to discuss perfectionism or making friends? How about a process through which students can learn appropriate expressions of emotions? You can tailor these lessons to fit the needs of your students. This unit is modeled from best practices for teaching gifted and talented students, who often live life thinking through metaphors (even if they don't know it yet).

Perhaps you've already taught Unit 1, which explores academic giftedness as a precious gift. Consider revisiting the topic as students return for a second semester of gifted and talented programming. Students will think critically about themselves and their abilities through a physical metaphor product—simple and fun to construct but packed with meaning. Graphic organizers and class discussions guide the class through the process. It's hands-on, thought-provoking, and fun. What more could students ask?

This unit provides examples to jumpstart a discussion about academic achievement and friendship, ready-to-print graphic organizers, a sample metaphor and how to construct it, an optional writing assignment, an extemporaneous speech application, and instructions for simple but effective student presentations.

Unit Objectives

Students will:
- » understand that people express what is inside their hearts through their words and actions, and
- » create a physical metaphor for important words and actions they use to express what is inside their own hearts.

NAGC Growth and Development Standards

1.2. Self-Understanding. Students with gifts and talents demonstrate understanding of how they learn and recognize the influences of their identities, cultures, beliefs, traditions, and values on their learning and behavior.

1.3. Self-Understanding. Students with gifts and talents demonstrate understanding of and respect for similarities and differences between themselves and their cognitive and chronological peer groups and others in the general population.

Themes and Skills Addressed

Social-Emotional Themes
- » Effort
- » Friendship
- » Compassion
- » Empathy
- » Identity
- » Psychosocial growth
- » Pride

Academic Skills
- » Collaborative discussion
- » Metaphor creation
- » Expository writing (optional)
- » Extemporaneous speaking

Figure 17
Works Progress Administration Poster

"January—A year of good reading ahead / Hazlett," 1936–1941, Chicago, IL, WPA Art Project. United States Library of Congress Prints and Photographs Division. https://www.loc.gov/pictures/item/98510133

Launch

Together as a class, view the Works Progress Administration poster shown in Figure 17. The image is available from the U.S. Library of Congress at https://www.loc.gov/pictures/item/98510133. If possible, project the image in color for all students to see.

The class does not necessarily need to reach any conclusions with this discussion. Rather, use the poster, questions, and discussion to encourage students to think about how words and images point to emotions and ideas. Questions and possible answers might include:

» What message do you take from this poster? *Reading is important and a good activity during the winter months when we might be stuck inside. Let's start the year off right with good books!*

» Why are the books so large? *They emphasize how important books and reading are.*

» Is it important that the person is walking uphill? *It shows that the books are important enough to the person that they are determined to pull them uphill through snow. Perhaps the hill symbolizes challenges ahead—difficulties that can be overcome with effort and persistence. This WPA poster was created between 1936 to 1941 during the Great Depression. It makes sense that the hill represents hard times ahead (or hard times that had been experienced in the past few years).*

» Is the person a boy or a girl? Could they be either one? Is that important for the message? *We don't know for sure if the person is a boy or a girl. It might be important that the person could be either one because that way both boys and girls can identify with the picture and will be encouraged to read.*

» Why is there an ellipsis after the word *good*? *The ellipsis invites us to read the poster in more than one way—that the "year" ahead will be good (even if it's an uphill climb) and/or that the "books" that will be read in the year ahead will be good.*

» Is there a reason *ahead* is a different color and so large? (Think back to Unit 2 and the emotional associations contained within different colors.) *Large print and a color stands out to signal importance The message helps us think about a good future ahead.*

Lesson 5.1

Qualities and Expression

The ultimate goal of this lesson is to help kids understand what is inside of themselves versus what characteristics they choose to express. Another way to look at it is *how you are* versus *what you do*.

As educators, we want our students to be caring, well-adjusted people who do good things in this world. Helping students understand the importance of being caring individuals is an important part of our job as gifted and talented resource teachers. Academic ability and potential are already present in gifted students. What these students do with that potential is what they express from the inside. This lesson can work toward both of these ends—social-emotional understanding and achievement.

Materials

- » Handout 5.1: What Comes From the Heart
- » Handout 5.1: What Comes From the Heart Sample

Estimated Time

- » 15 minutes

Procedure

Distribute Handout 5.1: What Comes From the Heart? Begin by providing a few examples together with the whole class. Here is your chance to tailor student responses to the graphic organizer by emphasizing certain qualities. For example, if you will be using this lesson to discuss how students might use their talents and abilities to express academic achievement, make sure "intelligence" and "abilities" are listed on the left side as internal qualities. Then place "hard work" and "doing your best" on the right side as ways a person might express these qualities. If you will use the lesson to discuss friendship, on the other hand, you might want to make sure "love" and "needs" appear on the left side, and "helping others" and "speaking kindly" on the right—using the right side to help students see different ways to make friends or to be a good friend.

Sample answers are included on the page following the handout.

NAME:_____ DATE: _____

Handout 5.1

What Comes From the Heart?

Directions: What are qualities that are inside of a person? What are qualities that people show others? On the left side of the organizer, place thoughts, feelings, and qualities people carry inside of them. Then, on the right, list ways that people show these thoughts, feelings, and qualities. The way that people show thoughts, feelings, and qualities is the way others understand what is on the inside.

In Someone's Heart	Comes From the Heart

NAME:_____ DATE: _____

Handout 5.1

What Comes From the Heart? Sample

Directions: What are qualities that are inside of a person? What are qualities that people show others? On the left side of the organizer, place thoughts, feelings, and qualities people carry inside of them. Then, on the right, list ways that people show these thoughts, feelings, and qualities. The way that people show thoughts, feelings, and qualities is the way others understand what is on the inside.

In Someone's Heart	Comes From the Heart
Intelligence	Trying hard
Ability	Doing your best
Love	Telling someone you are grateful
Fear	Avoiding other people
Generosity	Making a donation
Empathy	Helping others solve a problem

Social and Emotional Curriculum for Gifted Students, Grade 3 © Prufrock Press Inc.

Lesson 5.2

Defining Emotions and Qualities

In Lesson 5.2, students clarify their understanding of emotions or personal qualities by creating detailed definitions and providing examples. Students should express understandings that are *important to them* through metaphor. So, for example, although I might want to have a discussion about ability and achievement in my classroom, I understand it is more valuable for students to explore feelings and qualities inside their own hearts.

Materials

- » Handout 5.2: Wonderful Things Come From the Heart
- » Handout 5.2: Wonderful Things Come From the Heart Sample
- » Handout 5.2: Essay Prompt From the Heart (optional)
- » Handout 5.2: Essay Prompt From the Heart Sample (optional)

Estimated Time

- » 30 minutes

Procedure

As a class, using Handout 5.2: Wonderful Things Come From the Heart, discuss, define, and give examples of one of the qualities that "comes from the heart." For example, following an emphasis on achievement in this lesson, invite students to explore this topic further. Write "achievement" in the heart shape at the top. In a class discussion, have students provide both the definition and the examples to help complete the example. Don't stop here! All of this achievement talk from the teacher can be kind of boring. Use a second example that helps students think a little more about life and emotions—like the friendship example included in the sample pages that follow the handout.

Other suggested topics to explore include:

» resilience,
» effort,
» empathy,
» friendship,
» acceptance and understanding,
» hope, and
» pride (in the most positive sense).

Finally, invite each student to explore a topic they feel is important with their own graphic organizer, using Handout 5.2: Wonderful Things Come From the Heart. The goal is for students to think a little more deeply about how they interact with the world and where these thoughts and emotions come from.

Follow-Up: Optional Writing Activity

This lesson lends itself perfectly for an expository writing assignment. If you teach gifted students in a regular classroom setting or if you teach advanced literacy groups, you may want to use Handout 5.2: Essay Prompt From the Heart. This writing assignment is an excellent means for teaching students to answer questions with a clear statement, an explanation, and supporting details. Included is a sample response based on the topic of "effort."

Handout 5.2

Wonderful Things Come From the Heart

Directions: Choose a thought, feeling, or quality that comes from the heart. Define the quality and explain more about it by completing the graphic organizer below.

Thought, Feeling, or Quality:

Definition:

Example:

Example:

Example:

Handout 5.2

Wonderful Things Come From the Heart Sample

Directions: Choose a thought, feeling, or quality that comes from the heart. Define the quality and explain more about it by completing the graphic organizer below.

Thought, Feeling, or Quality:

Friendship

Definition:

Friendship is caring about another person and spending time with them. Friendship is understanding how another person acts and feels and knowing they understand the same about you. Friendship means taking the extra effort to show someone how much you like them.

Example:

Sometimes my friend can be kind of embarrassing or annoying—like when he says "moo" to just about everything I say! But that is part of the fun because he also makes me laugh.

Example:

I am always looking to play with my friend at recess. It doesn't matter what we play. It only matters that we are spending recess together. Some days I want to play soccer, but my friend really pretty much stinks at soccer. He still plays with me anyway. Some days I do things with him that I am not so good at.

Example:

I thought my friend was really cool, but this was before we were friends yet. I didn't know if he would think I was cool too. I would talk to him, and pretty soon we found out we had some things in common like drawing funny cartoons.

Social and Emotional Curriculum for Gifted Students, Grade 3 © Prufrock Press Inc.

Handout 5.2

Essay Prompt From the Heart

Directions: What is one wonderful quality that comes from the heart? Define the **quality and** provide an example that clarifies that quality.

_____

_____

_____

_____

_____

_____

_____

_____

_____

_____

_____

_____

_____

_____

_____

_____

_____

_____

_____

_____

_____

_____

Handout 5.2

Essay Prompt From the Heart Sample

Directions: What is one wonderful quality that comes from the heart? Define the quality and provide an example that clarifies that quality.

Effort is a wonderful quality that comes from the heart. Effort means trying your best and using your talents and abilities. Effort is putting in time to show your best even if putting in the effort doesn't always feel good. Effort means trying hard even at things you don't enjoy.

An example of effort could be found in a writing assignment. A student showing effort tries hard in writing even though it can be difficult. The student keeps working at the writing assignment even if they know they might have to make more edits and do another draft. It takes effort for success in things you are good at and for things you are not good at, too!

Social and Emotional Curriculum for Gifted Students, Grade 3 © Prufrock Press Inc.

Creating a Metaphor for Emotions and Qualities

Having completed the details for a quality that comes from the heart in the previous lesson, students are now ready to create a metaphor for this quality.

Materials

- » Handout 5.3: Concept Map: Creating a Metaphor
- » Handout 5.3: Concept Map: Creating a Metaphor Sample

Estimated Time

- » 15–20 minutes

Procedure

Creating the metaphor is the most difficult cognitive aspect of this unit and a powerful activity for gifted students. There is no perfect or foolproof way to create a metaphor. It always contains a mental leap, which even gifted kids can find to be a struggle.

Using a concept map helps with the process. It's simple, yet when students brainstorm words and phrases related to the quality they've chosen, images tend to meld together into a metaphor. Begin by examining a sample together as a class (see Handout 5.3 Concept Map: Creating a Metaphor Sample), continuing with the previous discussion of ability and achievement coming together through effort and persistence. Talk through the example as if you were creating it. What thoughts might be going through a person's mind while they are making connections? Explain how the conclusion of a fly caught in a web is reached.

Now it's the students' turn, individually, to undergo the same process with the concept they've chosen to transform into a metaphor. Make sure to circulate throughout the classroom and encourage students in what can be a frustrating process. Avoid providing any answers or solutions. The creation of a metaphor needs to spring from an individual's personal connections, and struggling with the process is healthy (as shown in the samples provided) and reflects strong higher order thinking skills for third graders.

Handout 5.3

Concept Map: Creating a Metaphor

Directions: What words and descriptions can you think of that relate to one of the qualities you've chosen that come from the heart? Complete the following concept map to help you.

Think about the words you've written in the ovals. What other item, situation, animal, etc., shares these descriptive words? This is your metaphor. Describe the metaphor in a few words.

_____

_____

_____

_____

_____

_____

Handout 5.3

Concept Map: Creating a Metaphor Sample

Directions: What words and descriptions can you think of that relate to one of the qualities you've chosen that come from the heart? Complete the following concept map to help you.

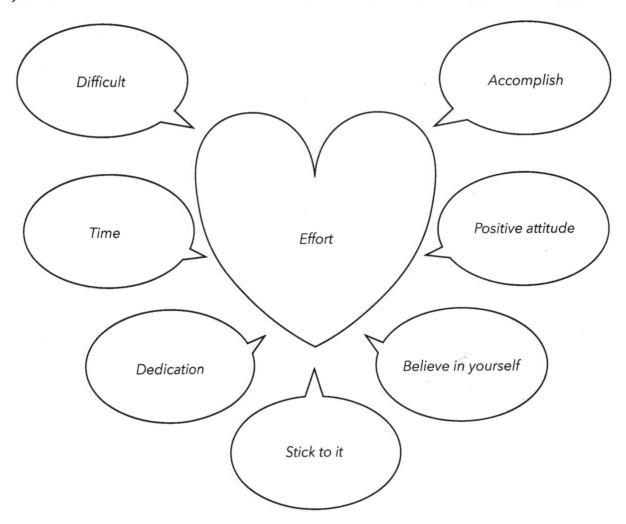

Difficult

Accomplish

Time

Effort

Positive attitude

Dedication

Believe in yourself

Stick to it

Think about the words you've written in the ovals. What other item, situation, animal, etc., shares these descriptive words? This is your metaphor. Describe the metaphor in a few words.

A fly trying to escape from a spider web.

Stick to it and keep trying even if it gets difficult!

Lesson 5.4

Constructing the Metaphor

Now that students have put in the most difficult think time already, they can get crafty! Get out the scissors, glue, and construction paper, and empty your junk drawer. It's time to build a project that shows what comes from the heart.

Materials

- » Handout 5.4: Extemporaneous Speaking Cards
- » Glue, tape, and scissors
- » Red construction paper (and other colors)
- » Cardstock
- » Various craft items or junk drawer items (e.g., beads, string, craft sticks, and odds and ends)

Estimated Time

- » 30 minutes, although the creative crafting process may take longer for some students

Procedure

Have students follow these steps to create their heart (see Figure 18 for step-by-step pictures):

1. Create a simple heart cutout using scissors and red construction paper. Fold a single piece of construction paper in half and cut the heart shape on the folded edge.
2. Cut out two long strips of cardstock—approximately 11 inches by 1 inch.
3. Tape one end of the cardstock strip to the other in an "L" shape.

129

4. Fold the strips together—back and forth and alternating—keeping the "L" shape with each fold. This will create a "springy thingy" from the two strips of paper (see photo in Step 4 of Figure 18).

5. Tape one end of the "springy thingy" onto the heart.

6. Make a physical representation of the metaphor you created in the previous lesson using the craft items. Try to make this three-dimensional instead of simply drawing a picture. Step 6 in Figure 18 shows a fly in a spider web to signify effort.

7. Attach the metaphor so that it literally "comes from the heart."

Follow-Up: Extemporaneous Speaking

Wrap up the lesson with brief student presentations. In these presentations, students should practice speaking extemporaneously from notecards and use their metaphors as a presentation aid. Students can simply hold up their product and explain the meaning of the metaphor.

These extemporaneous speeches are kid-sized, sweet, informative presentations, but they are also further practice in supporting an opinion with explanations and examples. Extemporaneous speaking is a skill that takes practice and is a good concept to introduce to challenge third graders.

Handout 5.4: Extemporaneous Speaking Cards provides notecards that students can complete and use to help them during their presentations.

Figure 18
Heart Construction Procedures

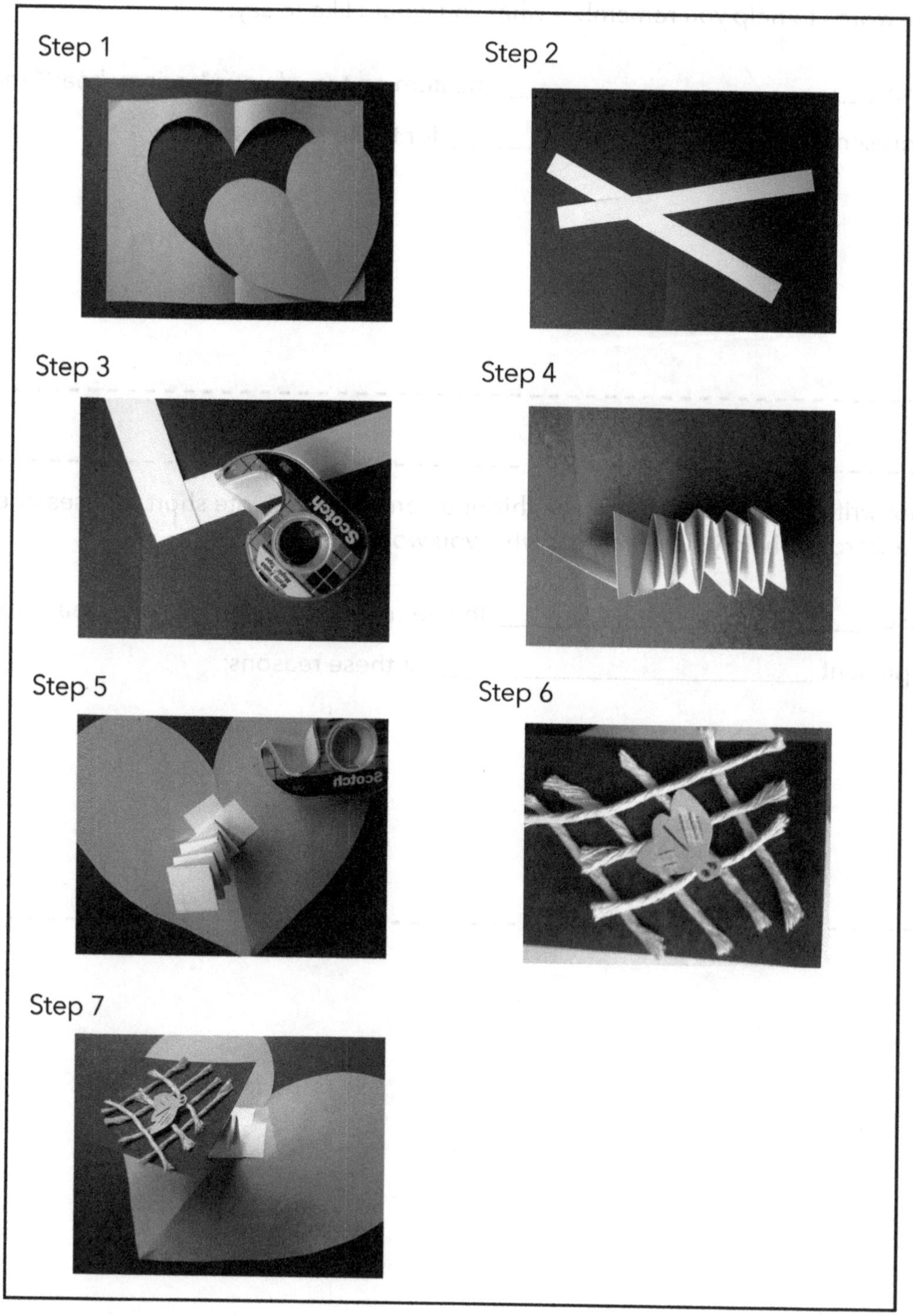

Step 1

Step 2

Step 3

Step 4

Step 5

Step 6

Step 7

Handout 5.4

Extemporaneous Speaking Cards

< UNIT 5: WHAT COMES FROM THE HEART >

Do not write complete sentences on this notecard. Instead write short phrases or even single words to help you remember what you would like to say.

I chose _____ (the item on top of your "springy heart" model)

to represent _____ for these reasons:

»

»

»

Do not write complete sentences on this notecard. Instead write short phrases or even single words to help you remember what you would like to say.

I chose _____ (the item on top of your "springy heart" model)

to represent _____ for these reasons:

»

»

»

Conclusion
Dear Gifted Learner

Collected in this section are various quotes and thoughts presented as short letters. Each is about life as a gifted learner in some way, and several are simply about life in general. Each letter opens discussion and allows students to pause and reflect in a mindful way—to slow down just a little bit and listen to their classmates' ideas and feelings.

I hope some of these letters inspire students to think ahead to all of the positive experiences they can build in their lives. A quote such as "You can change the future. Your opportunity comes every moment of every day" is, admittedly, not incredibly insightful. When this thought is shared and processed through the magic of synchronicity in a classroom, however, it can take on depth and power.

I also hope some quotes, on the other hand, produce a little ire. "Newsflash: Nobody wants to know how awesome you think you are" may raise some notes of indignation for your students, but it may just as well induce a little laughter. Indignation, ire, and laughter expressed in the safe atmosphere of your classroom lead to both engagement and impassioned discussion. Is this indignation felt because a student knows this quote does not describe them in the least, or has it hit a little too close to home? Either way, engaging with these words spurs self-discovery—maybe not exactly in that moment—but perhaps somewhere down the line. Gifted learners can often see another's perspective very clearly, and reminders of what are some of the most important aspects of life, like "Homework: Ask 10 people if a bigger heart or a bigger brain is more important," extend well beyond the classroom. In these ways, I hope these quotes and thoughts spur reflection, analysis, understanding, confluence, and some disagreement in a classroom climate that communicates acceptance and emotional safety. I hope everyone gets to hear some laughter, too.

These letters may be used as warm-ups with gifted students about once a week or so. Sometimes conversations may last 10 minutes, and sometimes 45 minutes. In my classroom, there have been times when we have returned to these discussions throughout the school year.

Thank you for taking care of our gifted learners.

NAGC Learning and Development Standards

1.1. Self-Understanding. Students with gifts and talents recognize their interests, strengths, and needs in cognitive, creative, social, emotional, and psychological areas.

1.2. Self-Understanding. Students with gifts and talents demonstrate understanding of how they learn and recognize the influences of their identities, cultures, beliefs, traditions, and values on their learning and behavior.

1.3. Self-Understanding. Students with gifts and talents demonstrate understanding of and respect for similarities and differences between themselves and their cognitive and chronological peer groups and others in the general population.

Themes and Skills Addressed

Social-Emotional Themes
- » Pride
- » Challenge
- » Identity
- » Executive functioning
- » What is giftedness?
- » Effort
- » Compassion
- » Empathy
- » Friendship
- » Resilience
- » Growth mindset

Academic Skills
- » Collaborative discussion
- » Inference

Dear Gifted Learner Letters Available Online

The Dear Gifted Learner Letters shared in this section may also be downloaded at https://www.prufrock.com/Social-and-Emotional-Curriculum-for-Gifted-Students-Resources.aspx.

Dear Gifted Learner Letters

Dear gifted learner,

If you have an idea about how to make your assignment more challenging, why not suggest it to your teacher?

Sincerely,

_____

Social and Emotional Curriculum for Gifted Students, Grade 3 © Prufrock Press Inc.

Dear gifted learner,

You may have amazing talents, but in the end, others only care if you are kind.

Sincerely,

_____

Social and Emotional Curriculum for Gifted Students, Grade 3 © Prufrock Press Inc.

Dear gifted learner,

Yes, behavior always matters.

Sincerely,

_____

Dear gifted learner,

No one has ever won an award for best normal.

Sincerely,

_____

Dear gifted learner,

Homework: Ask 10 people if a bigger heart or a bigger brain is more important.

Sincerely,

_____

Dear gifted learner,

You can change the future. Your opportunity comes every moment of every day.

Sincerely,

_____

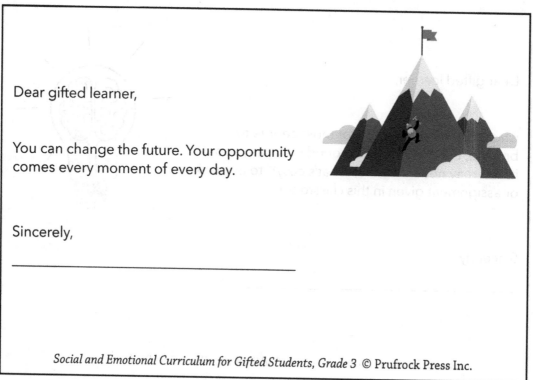

Dear gifted learner,

Class rule: You may not announce, "Done!" after completing assignments. Excellence does not equal speed. (Plus, it's annoying.)

Sincerely,

_____

Dear gifted learner,

Class rule: It's pretty easy for most people to breathe, but no one goes around bragging about it. You may not announce, "That's easy!" to any task or assignment given in this classroom.

Sincerely,

_____

Dear gifted learner,

Being humble means being so proud and so confident that you don't have to tell anyone about it.

Sincerely,

_____

Dear gifted learner,

Newsflash: Nobody wants to know how awesome you think you are.

Sincerely,

_____

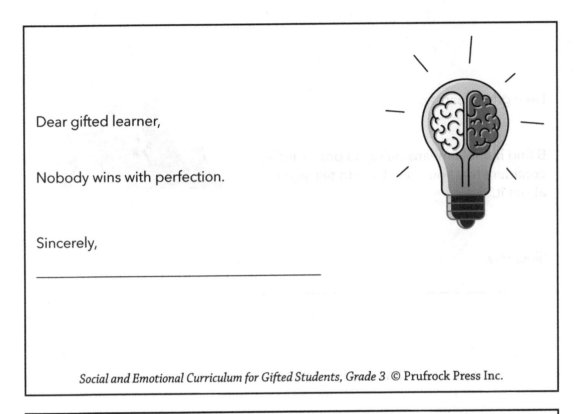

Dear gifted learner,

Nobody wins with perfection.

Sincerely,

_____

Social and Emotional Curriculum for Gifted Students, Grade 3 © Prufrock Press Inc.

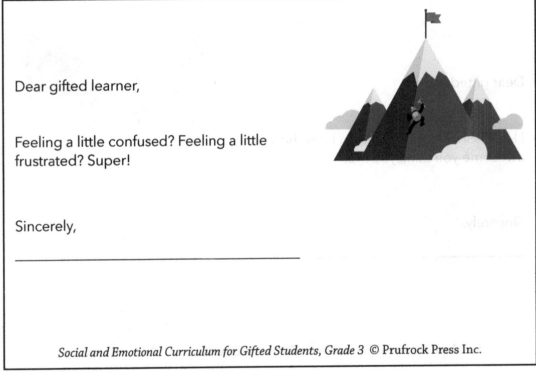

Dear gifted learner,

Feeling a little confused? Feeling a little frustrated? Super!

Sincerely,

_____

Social and Emotional Curriculum for Gifted Students, Grade 3 © Prufrock Press Inc.

Dear gifted learner,

How is your *today* going to become your *someday*?

Sincerely,

_____

Social and Emotional Curriculum for Gifted Students, Grade 3 © Prufrock Press Inc.

Dear gifted learner,

Choose one:
a. I am someone who believes they are better than others.
b. I am someone who believes they will never be good enough.
c. I am someone who always wants to be learning, growing, and meeting life's challenges with grace.

Sincerely,

_____

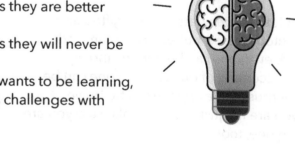

Answer: c. If you answered a. or b., erase really well or simply cross it out. Now change your answer to c. Congratulations! You are learning and growing gracefully.

Social and Emotional Curriculum for Gifted Students, Grade 3 © Prufrock Press Inc.

Dear gifted learner,

Class rules:
» Mistakes are encouraged.
» Experimentation is welcome.
» Creativity is highly regarded.

Sincerely,

_____

Dear gifted learner,

Not just *anyone* gets to be in gifted and talented classes, but *everyone* can work hard, *everyone* can be understanding and accepting of others, *everyone* can be generous, and *everyone* can be brave. If you are not just anyone, make sure you are everyone, too!

Sincerely,

_____

Dear gifted learner,

What if everyone understood that they can't save the world on their own but instead reached out to those nearby with kindness?

Sincerely,

_____

Dear gifted learner,

If you are the first one done, you may have had to try the least. When was the last time you heard famous artists, athletes, or musicians recognized for their excellence in trying the least?

Sincerely,

_____

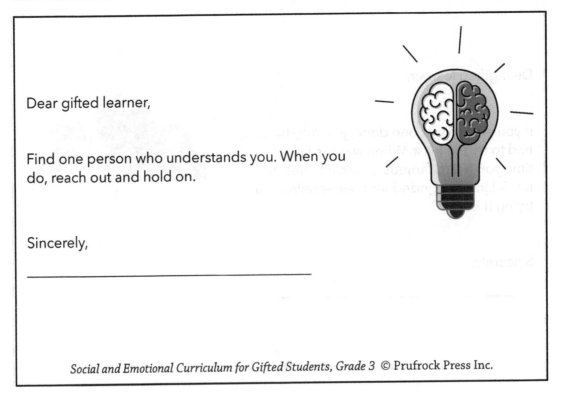

Dear gifted learner,

Try things you are not good at doing already.

Sincerely,

_____

Social and Emotional Curriculum for Gifted Students, Grade 3 © Prufrock Press Inc.

Dear gifted learner,

Find one person who understands you. When you do, reach out and hold on.

Sincerely,

_____

Social and Emotional Curriculum for Gifted Students, Grade 3 © Prufrock Press Inc.

Dear gifted learner,

Class rule: "A little weird" is a big compliment around here.

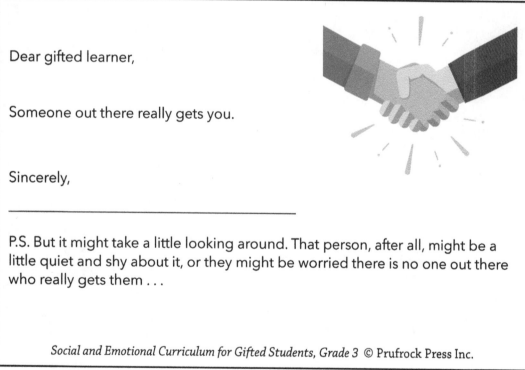

Sincerely,

_____

Dear gifted learner,

Someone out there really gets you.

Sincerely,

_____

P.S. But it might take a little looking around. That person, after all, might be a little quiet and shy about it, or they might be worried there is no one out there who really gets them . . .

References

Cohen, A. (2017). *This jigsaw puzzle was given to Ellis Island immigrants to test their intelligence.* Smithsonian Magazine. https://www.smithsonianmag.com/history/puzzle-given-ellis-island-immigrants-test-intelligence-180962779

Galbraith, J. (2013). *The survival guide for gifted kids* (3rd ed.). Free Spirit.

Dweck, C. S. (2016). *Mindset: The new psychology of success.* Ballantine Books. (Original work published 2006)

Hess, M. (2019). *Surfing a wave of wonderfulness.* National Association for Gifted Children. https://www.nagc.org/blog/surfing-wave-wonderfulness

National Association for Gifted Children. (2019). *2019 Pre-K–Grade 12 Gifted Programming Standards.* https://www.nagc.org/sites/default/files/standards/Intro%202019%20Programming%20Standards.pdf

Sumners, S., & Hines, M. E. (2020, August). Taking the creative leap: Thinking outside the "box." *Teaching for High Potential,* 19.

Sword, L. K. (2011). *Emotional intensity in gifted children.* Supporting the Emotional Needs of the Gifted. https://www.sengifted.org/post/emotional-intensity-in-gifted-children

About the Author

Mark Hess has spent more than 33 years teaching gifted learners. He is a gifted programs specialist in Colorado Springs, President-Elect for the Colorado Association for Gifted and Talented, and a member of the National Association for Gifted Children's advisory committee for *Teaching for High Potential* and NAGC's social-emotional needs committee. As a director on Supporting Emotional Needs of the Gifted's board, Mark is the senior associate editor of the SENG library. Visit Mark's website at https://www.giftedlearners.org to find free resources for parents and teachers to help meet the needs of gifted learners.